Blessings of The Holy Spirit

Marjorie Kann Jackson

Stillwater Books
A Division of Sycamore Creek Press
Fort Worth, Texas
stillwaterbooksus.com

We want to hear from you. Please send comments about this book to
contact@stillwaterbooksus.com. Thank you.

Stillwater Books
www.stillwaterbooksus.com
A Division of Sycamore Creek Press

Blessings of The Holy Spirit

Library of Congress Cataloging-In-Publication Data
Jackson, Marjorie Kann.
Blessings of the Holy Spirit/ Marjorie Kann Jackson
1st ed.
p. cm.
ISBN-13: 978-1484869048
1. Christian Living/Inspirational

First edition, Blessings Vol. 1, Stillwater Books 2013
Printed in the United States of America

For James Weldon Jackson

My husband
My life-long love
My best friend

*Thank you for providing me the freedom
to devote a lifetime to the study and
the teaching of God's word.*

Contents

Introduction

When my father, Dr. Herbert E. Kann, retired from 40 years as a Presbyterian minister he gave me the books he valued most. Dr. G. Campbell Morgan authored many of them. That was my introduction to Dr. Morgan's work.

Throughout the first 40 years of the 20th century Dr. Morgan was considered by many to be the greatest Bible expositor of that day. He explained the truths of Scripture as no one else could.

In 1904 he became pastor of Westminster Chapel in London, England. There were many requests that his sermons be made available in printed form. Each week Dr. Morgan chose one of his weekly messages for publication. At the end of the year they were bound under the title *The Westminster Pulpit.* I have 10 of those volumes. These lessons draw heavily on that body of work. They loosely follow his outlines and make use of his matchless word studies. I first taught them in Fort Worth, Texas, in 2009.

My life has been greatly enriched by Dr. Morgan's scholarship and by the insight the Holy Spirit gave to him. These lessons are my attempt to share these blessings with a new generation of seekers.

—*Marjorie Kann Jackson*

Invitation

Come now, and open the door to life change! Let your mind and heart slow their pace. Put aside for a little while the responsibilities of everyday, and join me here.

It has long been recognized that in order to live a life that is rich in spirit, we must become aware of the world that exists within ourselves. It is a world that is totally unseen, but every aspect of our outer world is governed by it and is an expression of it. Such inner worlds are built on a person's own truths. They are usually based on what can be seen and heard and touched and felt. They may express family patterns of thinking and responding or preconceived notions or insights. They may be the product of our education. At any rate, over time they faithfully reveal our interpretations of the circumstances and relationships that life confronts us with. Another way to say this is that the life that exists in us is the life that is lived out through us.

For many people this private world is filled with thoughts that chronically depress and defeat. They desperately seek escape from it; literally unable to bear the ideas that confront them there. Nothing is worse for them than times alone. Silence or solitude is torture. They busy themselves in work or play, in amusements or distractions, or numb or anesthetize themselves with food or drugs.

Some people have found a different way to live. It is in a inner world that is filled with peace and refreshment for soul and spirit; a world in which God Himself is our constant companion. Jesus spoke of this in *John 14:23.*

Jesus said, "If anyone loves me, he will obey my teaching. My Father will love him, and we will come to him and make our home with him."

In *Romans 12:2*, we read these words. *"And do not conform any longer to the pattern of this world, but be transformed by the renewing of your mind. Then you will be able to test and approve what God's will is, his good, pleasing and perfect will."* The Living translation of this verse reads, *"Be a new and different person with fresh newness in all you do and think."*

This book includes the following features.

SCRIPTURE REFERENCES ARE GIVEN IN THEIR ENTIRETY. Truth has many facets! As we look at it from different perspectives we gain new understanding. Just as a cut diamond reflects beauty in all its glory as it is examined from a number of angles, so the truth of Scripture acquires clarity and brilliance as we look at it from various viewpoints. In this book we provide you with that opportunity by including many Scripture references in their entirety so that you can experience Scripture commenting and expanding on Scripture.

MEMORIZATION. One Bible verse serves as the text for each lesson. It is suggested for memorization, for it encapsulates the primary teaching of that lesson.

PRAYER. At the end of each lesson you will find a prayer. These are the words of Prayer Songs that were given to me long ago. You can make them your own, or use them to lead you to the unique prayers of your heart. The Holy Spirit Himself is our teacher, and as we move into interactive study we want to invite His participation.

APPLICATION AND PRACTICE. Also at the end of each lesson you will find questions that will help you focus on the main points. They bring you to the heart of the learning process. They help you think through and practice what you are studying. They can be used for

11

individual meditation, and they are easily adaptable for group use. They encourage exploration and interaction.

A small group can serve as a valuable source of support, inspiration, and accountability. You may want to include time to worship together, to share experiences, to pray for one another, and to plan special activities. You will find pleasure in participating together in this journey!

PERSONAL JOURNALING. Throughout, you will find space to record your thoughts and insights. This will be a valuable aspect of the study, for it will make it uniquely your own. I suggest you purchase a small notebook to use in conjunction with the text. This will allow you to expand your notes and to collect ideas for meditation. I like to write my journal as a prayer to God. It is a wonderful way to simply talk to Him as to your very best friend.

May this book help you take one of the greatest truths of the Bible and bring to it a sharply defined understanding that is free of obscurity or confusion. Then you can adopt it as an integral part of the way you think and live.

To God be the glory!

Preface

For many centuries the world has recognized Easter as the high point of the Christian year. The resurrection of Christ from the dead is viewed as the dramatic culmination and definitive affirmation of the Truth of God as it is revealed through the Christian faith. However, there is more; much more! Here you will discover THE REST OF THE STORY.

Wonder of wonders, God loves us; and His Son set aside His prerogatives as God to come to earth and take upon Himself the heredity of sin and death that came to mankind through Adam. *1 Corinthians 15:22* expresses that truth in this way. *"For as in Adam all die, so in Christ all will be made alive."*

What is the heredity and the nature of sin? At its core it is my claim to my right to myself. It is my belief that I am my own God. *Romans 8:5-8* explains it this way. *"Those who live according to the sinful nature have their minds set on what that nature desires; but those who live in accordance with the Spirit have their minds set on what the Spirit desires. The mind of sinful man is death, but the mind controlled by the Spirit is life and peace. The sinful mind is hostile to God. It does not submit to God's law, nor can it do so. Those controlled by the sinful nature cannot please God."*

It was not out of sympathy that Jesus took upon Himself our sin. Rather, He bore it in order to put us back where God designed us to be: in union and in fellowship with Himself. God did not simply set our sin aside. He does not offer cheap forgiveness. Sin saddled us with a terrible debt; one we could never repay. That debt was

13

paid in full, because Jesus paid it all! Listen to the words of 2 *Corinthians 5:21.* *"God made him who had no sin to be sin for us, so that in him we might become the righteousness of God."*

Jesus rose from the dead, thus affirming the legitimacy of His claim to be the Son of God. He regenerates, putting into those who accept Him an inheritance of holiness.

Colossians 3:5 –10 enjoins us to *"Put to death, therefore, whatever belongs to your earthly nature: sexual immorality, impurity, lust, evil desires, and greed, which is idolatry. Because of these, the wrath of God is coming. You used to walk in these ways in the life you once lived. But now you must rid yourself of all such things as these: anger, rage, malice, slander, and filthy language from your lips. Do not lie to each other, since you have taken off your old self with its practices and have put on the new self which is being renewed in knowledge in the image of its Creator."*

Jesus completed this part of His mission by returning to heaven to ask The Father to send the Holy Spirit to be with all who put their faith in Him. As we shall see, that request was honored. The Holy Spirit is with us, and will be with us to the end of the age.

Foundational Texts

"The Lord will guide you always; he will satisfy your needs in a sun-scorched land and will strengthen your frame. You will be like a well-watered garden, like a spring whose waters never fail."

Isaiah 58:11

"On the last and greatest day of the Feast (of Tabernacles), Jesus stood and said in a loud voice, 'If anyone is thirsty, let him come to me and drink. Whoever believes in me, as the Scripture has said, streams of living water will flow from within him.' By this, he meant the Spirit, whom those who believed in him were later to receive. Up to that time the Spirit had not been given, since Jesus had not yet been glorified."

John 7:37–39

"And I will ask the Father, and he will give you another Counselor to be with you forever — the Spirit of truth. The world cannot accept him because it neither sees him nor knows him. But you know him, for he lives with you, and will be in you."

John 14:16–17

Peter replied, "Repent and be baptized, every one of you, in the name of Jesus Christ for the forgiveness of your sins. And you will receive the gift of the Holy Spirit. The promise is for you and your children and for all who are far off — for all whom the Lord our God will call."

Acts 2:38–39

Lesson One
Are You Living Out Of Your Flesh, Or Out Of Your Spirit?

TEXT: *"You, however, are controlled not by the sinful nature but by the spirit, if the Spirit of God lives in you. And if anyone does not have the Spirit of Christ, he does not belong to Christ."*

Romans 8:9, RV

The text for our lesson is found in *Romans 8:9*. This lesson will cover the first half of the verse, and the next lesson will cover the second half. In order to understand the context in which our text appears, we will begin by reading *Romans 8:1–9:*

> *"Therefore, there is now no condemnation for those who are in Christ Jesus, because through Christ Jesus the law of the Spirit who gives life has set you free from the law of sin and death. For what the law was powerless to do because it was weakened by the flesh, God did by sending his own Son in the likeness of sinful flesh to be a sin offering. And so he condemned sin in the flesh, in order that the righteous requirement of the law might be fully met in us, who do not live according to the flesh but according to the Spirit.*
>
> *Those who live according to the flesh have their minds set on what the flesh desires; but those who live in accordance with the Spirit have their minds set on what the Spirit desires. The mind governed by the flesh is death, but the mind governed by the Spirit is life and peace.*

The mind governed by the flesh is hostile to God;
it does not submit to God's law, nor can it do so.
Those who are in the realm of the flesh cannot
please God.

You, however, are not in the realm of
the flesh but are in the realm of the Spirit, if
indeed the Spirit of God lives in you. And if
anyone does not have the Spirit of Christ,
they do not belong to Christ."

In introduction, I would remind you that by His own declaration, Jesus Christ came into this world to save sinners. This was His self-proclaimed mission. *"I did not come to call the righteous, but sinners to repent." Matthew 9:13.* We are the sinners! We are not sinners because we sin. We sin because we are born sinners. Through Adam we receive our physical lives. Through Adam we are born of the flesh, but we are born with spirits that are dead.

What does that mean? How can that be? We look forward with joy to the birth of a precious baby. We hold that dear little one in our arms for the first time, and we rejoice in the occasion of the physical birth of this child. Yet Scripture tells us that even in that moment of ecstasy, death casts its shadow.

Genesis 2:15–17 says, "The LORD God took the man and put him in the Garden of Eden to work it and take care of it. And the LORD God commanded the man, 'You are free to eat from any tree in the garden; but you must not eat from the tree of the knowledge of good and evil, for when you eat from it you will certainly die.'" Note *Romans 5:12. "Therefore, just as sin entered the world through one man, and death through sin, in this way death came to all men … ".*

What is death? Death is not extinction, but separation. Physical death is the separation of the body from the soul and spirit. Spiritual death is the separation of the soul and spirit from God. We are born with spirits that are separated from the life of God. We have no way of extricating ourselves from this situation. It places us under the dominion of Satan. Jesus came to rescue us from the rule of Satan and from the kingdom of Satan and to restore us to the Kingdom of God. *Ephesians 2:1–10* outlines this truth, stating:

> *"As for you, you were dead in your transgressions and sins, in which you used to live when you followed the ways of this world and of the ruler of the kingdom of the air, the spirit who is now at work in those who are disobedient. All of us also lived among them at one time, gratifying the cravings of our flesh and following its desires and thoughts. Like the rest, we were by nature deserving of wrath. But because of his great love for us, God, who is rich in mercy, made us alive with Christ even when we were dead in transgressions — it is by grace you have been saved.*
>
> *And God raised us up with Christ and seated us with him in the heavenly realms in Christ Jesus, in order that in the coming ages he might show the incomparable riches of his grace, expressed in his kindness to us in Christ Jesus. For it is by grace you have been saved, through faith — and this is not from yourselves, it is the gift of God — not by works, so that no one can boast. For we are God's handiwork, created in Christ Jesus to do good works, which God prepared in advance for us to do."*

When God accomplishes all of this He also restores us to the balance and order and sanity that He ordained for our lives. This is a process that begins with our sins being forgiven and with our own spirits being literally born again. In *John 3:1–12* we find this explanation:

> *Now there was a Pharisee, a man named Nicodemus who was a member of the Jewish*

ruling council. He came to Jesus at night and said, "Rabbi, we know that you are a teacher who has come from God. For no one could perform the signs you are doing if God were not with him."

Jesus replied, "Very truly I tell you, no one can see the kingdom of God unless they are born again."

"How can someone be born when they are old?" Nicodemus asked. "Surely they cannot enter a second time into their mother's womb to be born!"

Jesus answered, "Very truly I tell you, no one can enter the kingdom of God unless they are born of water and the Spirit. Flesh gives birth to flesh, but the Spirit gives birth to spirit. You should not be surprised at my saying, 'You must be born again.' The wind blows wherever it pleases. You hear its sound, but you cannot tell where it comes from or where it is going. So it is with everyone born of the Spirit."

"How can this be?" Nicodemus asked.

"You are Israel's teacher," said Jesus, "and do you not understand these things? Very truly I tell you, we speak of what we know, and we testify to what we have seen, but still you people do not accept our testimony. I have spoken to you of earthly things and you do not believe; how then will you believe if I speak of heavenly things?"

We see here that life on earth affords us the opportunity to be born of God. All human beings are made by God. We are all His creation, but we are not all born of Him. That process involves the rebirth of our spirits. Jesus did not come to destroy our unique natures, but to take all that was polluted and ruined by sin and to forgive the sin and remake us in His image. That is accomplished as the Spirit of Christ comes to live in and through our born-again spirits. That is genuine transformation!

Years ago, James and I witnessed just such a change take place in a close friend. We met Bill when we were newly married, and he worked with James in the construction business. Some years passed, and before we knew it he and his wife had three children. We did too. By that time they had left Fort Worth, but we often visited back and forth on weekends.

As time passed, Bill became tense and verbally volatile with his family. After awhile, it wasn't much fun to be around them anymore. When they called about coming to spend the weekend with us, we didn't know what to expect. To our surprise, it became apparent that something wonderful had happened to Bill! He was unbelievably relaxed, patient, and kind with all six little children, and a delight to be with! James and I could hardly wait to get the children to bed to ask him what had happened. What had happened to change him so drastically?

Well, he had a story to tell. He had been teaching a Sunday-school class, and he gradually became aware that he wasn't the same person on Sunday morning that he was during the rest of the week. On Sunday, he had a smile on his face and a pleasant word for everyone. On Sunday, he worked hard to try to look and act like "a good Christian man." On Sunday, he put on his "Sunday-go-to-meeting" attitude along with his "Sunday-go-to-meeting" clothes; and off he went.

The spiritual crisis that changed his life, appeared on the surface to have been quite unremarkable, but it changed him forever. He told of how he was driving down a country road when it came to him that God didn't want his Sunday act. What God wanted was, as he put it,

"All of the dirty stinking parts of me so He could change them." Bill pulled over to the side of the road, and there he gave them all to God.

We keep in touch with our friends, and we can tell you that 50 years later Bill is still a man who was changed from the inside out by the power of God. I'm sure every one of you could tell similar stories. It is by no means unique, for that is what God wants to do for all of us. He wants to restore us to His divine ideal. What is that ideal?

Keeping that question in mind, let's look again at our text. Note that in the very middle of this verse, we encounter a word that is startling. It is the little word *"if."* Let's take a look at it. *"You, however, are controlled not by the sinful nature but by the spirit, IF the Spirit of God lives in you."* This is the divine ideal! God's plan is for the Spirit of God to come live in us! Isn't that amazing?

On the other hand, it is entirely possible to live without the Spirit of God. People live entire lifetimes without the Spirit of God in them. They may call themselves Christians. They may attend church every Sunday. They may contribute generously to their church. They may sing in the choir. They may even be teachers or preachers. But the Spirit of God does not live in them.

What takes place when the Spirit of God comes to live in us? In order to answer that question I want to draw your attention to a simple difference in spelling that we find within our text. In many of the Bible translations we find that the word *"spirit"* is almost always spelled with a capital letter. In the Revised Version, the word *"spirit"* is often spelled with a lower case letter. It is of great importance to examine this difference if we are to correctly understand what was in the mind of the apostle Paul when he wrote these words. Much of the message of this lesson rests on a correct understanding of this.

We see that the word *"spirit"* appears three times in our text. In most of the versions we have today, the word is spelled with a capital "*S*" in all three places. According to that spelling, in every case, the apostle was referring to the Spirit of God, to the Spirit of Christ, to the Holy Spirit. Let us see what that would mean.

"You, however, are controlled not by the sinful nature but by the Spirit (the Holy Spirit) if the Spirit of God lives in you, and if anyone does not have the Spirit of Christ, he does not belong to Christ."

However, in the Revised Version, the first time the word "*spirit*" occurs, it is not capitalized. That changes the meaning completely. Let's see what that means.

"You, however, are controlled not by the sinful nature but by the spirit (your own spirit) if the Spirit of God lives in you." How are we to understand this? What does it mean for us? What difference does it make?

Dr. Morgan did a long and detailed study of this entire passage. He came to accept without reservation the spelling of the Revised Version because he believed it to offer the most accurate interpretation. That may surprise us, for if we accept that, we are brought to some important questions concerning the nature of our own spirits. What is our spirit? What is the purpose of our spirit?

Two Biblical terms reveal the nature of every person. Those terms are "*flesh*" and "*spirit*." They reveal us to be material and immaterial beings. The fleshly side of our life is the side that can be seen. Our soul and spirit make up the part of us that cannot be seen. In *I Thessalonians 5:23* Paul prays for the sanctification of the entire human being in these words; "*May your whole spirit and soul and body be kept blameless.*" Spirit, soul, and body: this is the three-fold fact of human existence. Made in the image of God, there is a three-fold oneness.

Our souls contain our unique personalities including our emotions and our wills. Through our bodies and using our five senses, our souls communicate with the material world. Our spirits hold within them the spiritual part of our being. God's plan was that our lives be controlled by our own spirits as they were indwelt by the Spirit of God and were in communication with Him. However, as we have already noted, back in the Garden of Eden Adam and Eve experienced spiritual death. Because of sin their spirits were separated from the Spirit of God. Their own spirits, that had been filled with the Life of God, now became death chambers. You can read the story of Adam and Eve in *Genesis 3*.

There is an understanding of our humanity that lies behind the great statement of our text. It is that our spirit is the most important thing about us. Paul understood that, and he also understood something beyond that. He understood the great truth that we choose the sphere out of which we will live. We can choose to live out of that side of our nature that is of the flesh, or we can choose to live out of that side of our nature that is of the spirit. Let's notice the contrast that exists between them.

In *2 Peter 1:9*, Peter wrote that those who live out of the flesh *"cannot see afar off."* They are nearsighted. They only see the things that are near. They only see the things of this world. The person living in the flesh cannot see or hear or understand the voice that speaks to us of eternity. That person believes that those who hear spiritual things are deceived or are fanatics. However, whatever path the one living out of the flesh chooses it ultimately leads to disappointment and darkness and death in all its forms. *Romans 7:4–6* bears this out.

> *"So, my brothers and sisters, you also died to the law through the body of Christ that you might belong to another, to him who was raised from the dead, in order that we might bear fruit for God. For when we were in the realm of the flesh, the sinful passions aroused by the law were at work in us, so that we bore fruit for death. But now, by dying to what once*

bound us, we have been released from the law
so that we serve in the new way of the Spirit,
and not in the old way of the written code."

In *Matthew 6:23* we read, *"If the light that is in you is darkness, how great is that darkness."* This is the experience of those who live out of their flesh. They experience a hunger within their own spirits that cannot be satisfied. They live with a spiritual thirst that they cannot quench. Their life is marked with the presence of a nameless and constant fear. It dogs every step. At last, there comes the awareness that there is no satisfaction to be found for the burning desire of their hearts. No material possession will quench that fire. No amount of money can buy freedom. No level of education can satisfy their spirits. No earthly relationship brings a permanent sense of completion. There is nowhere to turn. There is nowhere to run. There is nowhere to hide. Where does this road lead?

It leads to hardness of heart. It paves the way to a life in which faith and hope are finally lost. It leads to questions that may remain forever unanswered. That is life as it is lived out of the flesh, for those who live out of the flesh mind the things of the flesh. Their minds are set on the things of the flesh. *"What shall we eat? What shall we drink? How shall we be clothed?"* *Matthew 6:31.* What will bring us pleasure? Their minds are occupied with the things of the flesh every day and every night.

The Apostle Paul has more to say about a mind set on the things of the flesh. He says that the mind set on the flesh cannot please God. It is not subject to the law of God, for it prefers its own ideas. The life lived out of the flesh is a life that is lived as if there were no God and as if there were no eternity. It is a life that is lived as if no world exists but this present one. It is a life that is lived as if death is the end of it all.

Romans 8:1–17 tells us a lot about life lived out of the flesh and life lived out of the spirit. We have already looked at verses 1-9. Here we will read *Romans 8:10–13.*

"But if Christ is in you, then even though your body is subject to death because of sin, the Spirit gives life because of righteousness. And if the Spirit of him who raised Jesus from the dead is living in you, he who raised Christ from the dead will also give life to your mortal bodies because of his Spirit who lives in you. Therefore, brothers and sisters, we have an obligation — but it is not to the flesh, to live according to it. For if you live according to the flesh, you will die; but if by the Spirit you put to death the misdeeds of the body, you will live. For those who are led by the Spirit of God are the children of God. The Spirit you received does not make you slaves, so that you live in fear again; rather, the Spirit you received brought about your adoption to sonship. And by Him we cry, 'Abba, Father'. The Spirit Himself testifies with our spirit that we are God's children. Now if we are children, then we are heirs — heirs of God and co-heirs with Christ, if indeed we share in his sufferings in order that we may also share in his glory."

From our perspective, there are gradations of life lived out of the flesh. We see people who give themselves over to the most awful passions and behaviors, and that is life lived out of the flesh. There are also people who are living out of the flesh who try to live good and honorable lives. They may acknowledge God, but reject Jesus. That is because their own ideas about ultimate salvation trump God's. If it comes down to the ideas touted in the latest *New York Times* bestseller versus the teachings of the Bible, guess which one wins out? They may profess to pray to God, but in their prayers they seek their own will and way. They do not recognize any reality except the reality of today. In the eyes of heaven it is all life on the same fleshly, self-centered, self-determined level.

Let it be said that if there were no God and no life beyond the grave, then we would make a great difference between these two categories. There would be the difference that exists between what is respectable and what is obscene and offensive. However, here we are not making such a differentiation. Here we are looking at life in the light of the Biblical message. If we want to compare a higher life with a lower life we can't do it by comparing flesh with flesh. We must compare the life of the flesh with the life of the spirit.

Let's look at the life lived out of the spirit. Those who live with this perspective understand that this life affords us a time of preparation for eternity. We know that it is in eternity that our lives will come to their complete fulfillment. The question is, what takes place here and now when we choose to live out of the spiritual side of our nature? We are given a new vision of God and a new vision of life. In Hebrews, we read an interesting comment on life lived out of the spirit. *"He endured as seeing Him Who is invisible."* *Hebrews 11:27.* This was spoken of Moses, but it could just as well be spoken of people who are living today.

Those who live out of the flesh can't understand this. What in the world does it mean? They may just smile tolerantly, or they may ridicule aloud. How do we know that someone sees the invisible? We know by the way they endure! Courageous endurance demonstrates far vision. This quotation comes to us from days of old, but women sit here with us today who see Him who is invisible. They know that wherever they are and whatever is happening, God is here; and so they endure — as seeing.

Those who live out of the spirit experience life indeed! They have eyes that can see and ears that can hear and hearts that can understand. They know ecstasy and power. They know joy and peace; and they know courage and bravery which enables them to endure.

Notice here what our text reveals about the one who lives out of the spirit. *"You are not in the flesh but in the spirit, if_____."* We pause once again at that *"if."* How can we cross that line from living out of the flesh to living out of the spirit? And the answer is given to us, *"If the Spirit of God dwells in you."* It is up to us to invite Him in!

The Spirit of God is given to restore us to a true relationship with God and to restore balance and proportion to our lives so that they will bring honor and glory to Him. Are we living out of the flesh or out of the spirit? It is easy to make that determination. Just answer the following questions. What is life all about? What claims our time, our money, and our effort? What determines our truth and our perspective? Finally, is life all about us?

If that is how we are living, we are living out of our flesh. We are living inverted lives! The Spirit of God wants to take our lives and turn them completely around. He will transform us! He will make us over in the sense of reversal. He will bring us back into harmony with God. More and more, we will experience a oneness with Him. In accomplishing this, He brings us back to the meaning of our own being and existence. Consider *2 Corinthians 3:17–18. "Now the Lord is the Spirit, and where the Spirit of the Lord is, there is freedom. And we all, who with unveiled faces contemplate the Lord's glory, are being transformed into his image with ever-increasing glory, which comes from the Lord, who is the Spirit."*

Our text recognizes these facts. The choice is ours and we cannot avoid it. We can live with our eyes and ears closed to the infinite and with no awareness of the nearness of God. On the other hand, we can choose to live out of our spirits; seeing what others do not see, hearing what others do not hear, and accepting revelations that, apart from God, cannot be discovered.

If we are living out of our flesh, how can we escape such a life? How can we cross the line that exists between lives lived out of the flesh and lives lived out of the spirit?

We cross that line when we accept the new birth that God offers us through faith in the Lord Jesus Christ. We cross that line when the Spirit of God is welcomed into our lives. His coming heralds our new birth. He restores our dead spirits to life. From that very moment, we enter into a new relationship of communication and communion with God. We are given a new consciousness of the far things. We live no longer in slavery to our flesh. Rather, our own spirits, indwelt by the Spirit of Christ, are placed in control of our lives. The change is brought about as we enter into the Life of the Spirit of God.

This is the test of our profession of Christianity. We can memorize Scripture. We can recite prayers. We can read our Bibles from cover to cover; but if we are living out of the flesh we come under the condemnation of God. When we choose to live out of our flesh, we are not living up to the wonderful possibilities God has ordained for our natures. We are not living up to the potential of our personalities. It is not possible to live human life to its fullest if we are living out of our flesh.

Let me tell you that there is one thing you absolutely cannot do if you are living out of the flesh. You dare not think on these things! The one thing you dare not do is think! You must stay busy! You must cram your life full of activities and noise. There must be noise from morning till night with television, radio, iPods, and CDs. Glaring lights! Clashing music! We will use anything to distract us from the disappointments, deterioration, degeneration, doom, dying, and damnation. That is not life! Oh, that we might see for ourselves the absolute horror of it! That is how many people try to live.

We were made to lift our faces to God! God has put eternity into our hearts, and time can never satisfy the call of eternity. The life of our souls and of our spirits can never be satisfied with the things of this world. Nothing but unbroken fellowship can satisfy the heart of either man or God. Communion with Him is the highest blessing on earth as well as in heaven.

The Spirit of God waits to enter into a personal relationship with the spirit of every person. God brings His own Life and Strength into my spirit, making my spirit dominant in my life just as He intended it should be from the beginning. From that moment on, my flesh can serve my spirit. My flesh no longer is my master.

This is the way of a full life. My spirit exists in fellowship with the Spirit of God! Then what? What does that look like? What does that feel like? From that time on, it is possible for my flesh to be directed and inspired by the Spirit of God as I surrender to Him. Through my flesh, my spirit will communicate with God, with His world, with His children, with time, and with eternity.

Is it possible to live such a life? Is it really possible? Do we all have the ability and the opportunity to leave behind us forever the life we lived in the flesh and enter fully into the life of our spirit? It is absolutely possible, and it is accomplished by receiving the Holy Spirit. He comes to live in us when our dead spirits are born again.

There is a wonderful story in the Gospel of John. In *John 7:37–38*, Jesus stood in the midst of the crowds at the Feast of Tabernacles, and He said, *"If anyone thirsts, let him come to Me and drink. He that believes on Me, as the Scripture has said, out of his inner life shall flow rivers of living water."*

Well, what did He mean by that? What was He talking about? The next verse tells us. *"This spake He of the*

Spirit, which they that believed on Him were to receive; for the Spirit was not yet given; because Jesus was not yet glorified."

That declaration had a historic application and a personal application. Historically, it meant that until Jesus was glorified by way of His death and resurrection, the Spirit could not come. The personal application is that Jesus must be glorified in our own lives. We must receive Him as our Lord and Savior, and then we must glorify Him with our love. We must glorify Him with our trust. We must glorify Him with our obedience. We must glorify Him by surrendering our life to Him. Then what? The answer to our faith in Christ is God's gift to us of the Holy Spirit.

How much do we trust Him? How truly do we believe in Him? How much do we yield to Him? Yielding to His Spirit is a day-by-day proposition. His mercies are new every morning. Our surrender must be fresh and new every day.

Then what? Day by day we discover that life is new and different and dynamic. We find ourselves living "as seeing Him Who is invisible." My mother wrote down in her Bible what that felt like to her. She wrote, "The happiest, healthiest, most exciting, most rewarding life possible!"

Make Known Your Majesty

Make known to us Your majesty
As we gather in this place;
And reveal to us Your presence
As together we seek Your face.

For as You came down from glory
To save us from the fall;
And as You showed us the Father,
Then gave Your Life for all,
May we hide Your truth within us,
And leave behind our wrongful ways;
May we humbly rise to meet Your call
And joyfully serve You all our days.

Make known to us Your will, O Lord
As we follow in Your ways,
And fill us with Your Spirit
As together we seek Your grace.

We will glory in Your presence
As we gather 'round Your throne;
And we'll sing alleluias to the Lamb
All praise be to our God alone!

Think On These Things

Do you know anyone whose life was genuinely transformed by their surrender to the Holy Spirit? What did you notice about that?

Have you experienced that kind of transformation? Are you able to share what that was like?

Why is your spirit the most important thing about you?

What do you think it means to live out of your flesh?

How can you live out of your spirit?

Where do you look for "light"?

Where are you trying to quench your thirst? Look at what is claiming your time and effort and money. Look at your checkbook and your calendar. That will help you find your answer.

When was the last time you consciously surrendered to God and His ways? Can you share what that was like for you?

Does the Spirit of the Living God live in you? How do you know the answer to that question?

I think you will enjoy reading and thinking about *1 Corinthians 2:6–16.*

Lesson Two
The Ultimate Test of Christianity

TEXT: *"You, however, are controlled not by the sinful nature but by the spirit, if the Spirit of God lives in you. And if anyone does not have the Spirit of Christ, he does not belong to Christ."*

Romans 8:9, RV

Romans 8:9 is once again our text. This verse is recognized by many scholars to stand as the supreme test of Christianity. In the last lesson our attention was confined to the first part of the verse. Now we are going to consider the second part. In our last lesson we examined this verse in its context by reading *Romans 8:1-9*. You may want to turn back and reread those verses.

When we look at *Romans 8:9* in its entirety, we notice immediately a change in its expressions. We note the expression, *"the Spirit of God"*; and we note the expression *"the Spirit of Christ"*. Both of these expressions are referring to the Holy Spirit, and that makes this change of expression more intriguing. Why the change? Some scholars have understood the second phrase, *"the Spirit of Christ"*, as a reference to the disposition, the nature, and the character of Christ. In that case it could be read, *"If any man has not the disposition of Christ, the nature of Christ, the character of Christ, he is none of His."*

Dr. Morgan believed that to be the significance of this change in expression. Understanding both references to be to the Holy Spirit, Dr. Morgan felt that, in the change of wording the writer sought to point out that the Spirit of Christ in us produces the mind of Christ and the disposition of Christ in us. The result of the Spirit of Christ in us will be outwardly demonstrated in our character. What is in us will be demonstrated through us. The expression *"the Spirit of Christ"* points us to the result of His indwelling; to the outcome of His indwelling as it is seen and observed by others.

So what is the significance of the first expression, *"the Spirit of God"*? This expression refers to the Spirit as a mighty force. It would remind us of the hidden, unseen power of the Spirit of God; of the mighty power that raised Jesus from the dead.

The life of Jesus was filled with beauty and glory, and its secret was that He lived in constant fellowship with the Spirit of God. Jesus was born of the Spirit. The Spirit protected and sustained His life. The Spirit led him into the wilderness. He returned to do His work in the power of the Spirit. Finally, through the Spirit, Jesus offered Himself without blemish to God. He acted in constant co-operation with the indwelling Spirit of God. He never resisted the Spirit. He never grieved the Spirit. He never quenched the Spirit. And what resulted from living such a life? The Spirit of God was seen through the Spirit of Jesus. Jesus said, *"He who has seen me has seen the Father."* *John 14:9.* As we consider these two phrases, *"the Spirit of God"* and *"the Spirit of Christ"*, we will discover that they bring us to consider things seen and things unseen in the Christian life and character.

Once again we find ourselves treading on Holy Ground. One of my students said to me after a class, "I don't know anyone who is even considering these things. I don't know anyone who is teaching these things."

To the extent that this is true may God have mercy on us, for as we explore the second half of this verse we will see that it will test our Christianity, it will measure our commitments, it will propose balances, and finally it will reveal clearly whether or not we have the Spirit of God.

Hold firmly in mind that the absence of the Spirit of Christ demonstrates the absence of the Spirit of God. The presence of the Spirit of Christ demonstrates the presence of the Spirit of God. Those are the simplest of statements, but in all of the writings of Scripture they propose perhaps the most searching of tests.

We are going to pause now to consider the nature and the importance of a person's character. Character is what we are and what others see. Character cannot be expressed by the things that we say or by the things that we do. Does that surprise you? Many have thought that those are the very things that reveal character! However it is true that the most vulgar person may use the language of sainthood. The most self-centered and egotistical person may make the largest gifts to charity. It is not the things that we say or do which, in the final analysis, tell the tale. Our character is revealed through our disposition. Our character is what we are!

A godly character may be measured by the Sermon on the Mount, by the Beatitudes, and by the fruit of the Spirit; but the fact is that only God knows the truth of a person's character.

That is why we all need times alone with Him, times in which we ask Him to search our spirits and look into our souls. *"Search me, God, and know my heart; test me and know my anxious thoughts. See if there is any offensive way in me, and lead me in the way everlasting." Psalm 139:23–24.* That is when we may find out whether we belong to Christ or not.

Now, let us turn our attention to the character of Jesus. What did others see in Him? What was the temper, the tone, the disposition, and the quality of the Spirit of God as it was revealed through Him? In order to answer those questions, we want to inquire at the human level. Very quickly we will recognize that these questions do not have simple answers.

If we ask about the words that He spoke, we can fairly easily refer to them. We recognize their spiritual value. We know we will never be able to plumb their depths. If we ask about what He did, we can follow the path He walked. We can follow the thread of His deeds. We can read of the miracles He performed. But it is more difficult to see the Spirit of Christ.

What can we say about it? As we read the well-known stories of His life, what can we glean as to His character? Dr. Morgan suggests three words that characterized His life — simplicity, sensitivity, and serenity. He lived a life of simplicity rather than complexity. He lived a life of sensitivity rather than callousness, and He lived a life of serenity rather than chaos.

What do I mean when I speak of a life of simplicity? Jesus was always honest, straightforward, natural, transparent, and simple. What you saw was what He was. Complexity can easily turn into hypocrisy. The Spirit of Jesus was simple in that it was free of all pretense and free of all sin.

He spoke freely concerning His inner life. He said astounding things that, if spoken by other men, would have seemed the epitome of egotism. Standing one day in the midst of a hostile, angry crowd, Jesus said, *"I always do the things that are pleasing to God."* John 8:29. If one of our pastors made such a declaration, what would be our response? We might well be incredulous!

How could anyone say that? And yet we read in many places in the Gospel of John that, *"As He spoke these things, many believed on Him." John 8:30.* People were deeply touched by His simplicity, His honesty, and His transparency.

He said, *"I am the Truth."* The message was not that He preached the truth, or expounded on the truth, or taught the truth, or held to the truth. Rather, the message was *"I am the Truth."* He had no secrets. There were no hidden areas of His life. Simplicity is not superficial. It is transparent. All that is there can be seen clearly.

In trying to think of an example that would be meaningful to me, I remembered a place where our family vacationed on the shore of Lake Superior. The water of that lake is cold and crystal clear. Below our cabin was a great pool of shallow water, and we could see right through it to the beautiful rocks that were lying on the bottom. My little brother and I spent some happy hours collecting those rocks. The Spirit of Jesus, the character of Jesus, the disposition of Jesus was absolutely clear and transparent and simple. It was possible to see the beauty that lay beneath the surface! The nature of God and the methods He uses in dealing with us are profound in their simplicity. He opens our eyes to the beauty and truth of the spiritual realm.

Now we come to the quality of sensitivity. Jesus freely shared in the emotions of others. When He found Himself confronted by sorrow, He took that sorrow into Himself. When He encountered the brokenhearted and widowed mother following her only son to burial, He felt the sorrow of her heart. When He went to the marriage feast at Cana of Galilee He felt keenly the gladness and joy of the occasion. He was deeply responsive. He was acutely sensitive.

Then, what about the serenity of Jesus? As we see Him in Scripture, we find that when all around Him were agitated and excited, He alone remained calm and quiet and filled with dignity. Many scenes come to our minds, but none quite as poignant and powerful as those final hours before His crucifixion. Rome, with the power it held to rule with an iron fist, was thrown into chaos. The priests were aroused to a white heat. The disciples were confused and fearful. The population was clamoring for blood. The only Spirit that displayed calmness and serenity was the Spirit of Christ.

In the midst of the total disorder and catastrophes that life holds He is still the serene one, unafraid and unmoved. We often become excited or discouraged or fearful. In contrast, Jesus' life demonstrated serenity. He was filled with the powerful serenity of God!

The question we need to consider is whether or not our lives reflect these characteristics; simplicity, sensitivity, and serenity. Lacking them, we lack the Spirit of Christ. Lacking the Spirit of Christ, we lack the Spirit of God, for He always produces in human lives these same manifestations. And that brings us to the statement in the last part of *Romans 8:9. "If any man does not have the Spirit of Christ, he is none of His."*

We see that this is serious business, so how are we to apply this test? This involves divine examination and that is different in method from human examination. Tests of the spirit are not announced ahead of time. We are not given the date and time when the test will be given. We are not given special time to prepare. Tests may come to us in the course of an ordinary day, or they may come in the guise of an unexpected crisis. Always, we discover what kind of spirit we have by way of our commonplace and everyday responses.

It is important to understand that the tests are not given for God's benefit. He knows my mind. He knows my heart. He knows my nature and my character. He knows what my responses will be, so the tests are not for

Him. They are always for me. They reveal to me who I am. They show me the spirit that is in me.

We can't discover here around this table whether or not we have the Spirit of Christ. The discovery is made within the routines and challenges and habits of everyday living. Our spirits are tested in the large and the small issues of life. They are tested through victory, and they are tested through defeat. They are tested in prosperity, and they are tested in adversity. They are tested in sickness and they are tested in health. Popularity tests them. Obscurity tests them. We are tested in a thousand small ways as the busy hours or the empty hours of every day unfold.

How are our spirits tested? When storms of adversity are sweeping over us, when it seems that all things are against us, that is the time of testing. Some people give way to despair. Others practice patient endurance. Some people are fretful and filled with worry and fear. Others are calm and peaceful. Some express dissatisfaction and resentment. Others, in the same circumstances accept what God allows with the confident expectation that out of it God will bring unimagined good.

"And we know that in all things God works for the good of those who love him, who have been called according to His purpose. For those God foreknew He also predestined to be conformed to the image of His Son, that he might be the first born among many brothers and sisters." Romans 8:28–29 KJV. What is the difference? It is the difference of disposition, and the disposition reveals whether we are living out of the flesh or out of the spirit.

It is not only adversity that tests us. Our spirits are also tested when success marks our path, when all is succeeding, when everything is going well. At such a time there are people who become arrogant and overbearing. They show contempt for those who fail. They use their success to tear down and undermine others. They become proud, taking credit for their accomplishments and for what they see as their superior insight and wisdom. On the other hand, there are those people who grow ever more humble as success comes their way, and they give God the glory for it. They freely share their good fortune. They reach out and try to use their position and influence and resources to help others.

What determines the difference? The difference lies within their soul and spirit. It lies within their disposition. There is a very real sense in which neither person can help what they are doing, for we all do what we are! Our lives reveal the truth of what is in us.

The common events of every day faithfully reveal the spirit that controls us. The keys that cannot be found at the last minute, the bill that was not mailed on time, the burned toast, the everyday frustrations — these small events will quickly demonstrate what controls our lives. Our text reminds us, *"If any person does not have the Spirit of Christ, he is none of His."*

I am not your judge. I do not ask you to accept my opinion of you. I do not ask you to accept the opinion of either friend or foe, and I do not accept your judgment of me. We all will stand or fall before our own master. In the deepest part of my inner life I stand at the judgment seat of Christ; and I know that the responses of my soul and spirit reveal the truth concerning my relationship to Him.

I think our text would scare me to death if it were not for the first part which we considered in our last lesson. After all, if our Christianity is not to be tested by our creed but by our spirits, aren't we all guilty? The questions rise up within us! How can we have the Spirit of Christ? How is it that we become like Him? How can we find our way to simplicity, to transparency, and to absolute truth? How can we leave hypocrisy behind? How can we move beyond the panic that suddenly seizes us? How can we stop the frantic activity that marks our days? How can we get away from the callousness that has caused us to be unable to cry when confronted with sorrow and unable to laugh in the presence of joy? How can we find for ourselves the calmness, the serenity, and the confident peace of Christ? How can we escape lives that have been mastered by the flesh and controlled by the self? How can we find the Spirit of a God-centered life?

That inquiry is answered in the first part of our text. *"You are not in the flesh but in the spirit, if the Spirit of God lives in you."* We see right here that by controlling the external aspects of our lives, we cannot create a godly spirit. We cannot create a godly spirit by promising ourselves that we will never speak a cross word again. We may be able to keep that promise for a while, but if our spirit is unkind, we will eventually find ourselves responding with poisoned words. Our spirits will never be made over by our changing external things. Our spirits will not be transformed by our efforts to reform what we say or what we do. Change will have to come from the inside out.

We also need to understand that imitation does not produce the Spirit of Christ in us. As I think on the simple, sensitive and serene Christ, I admire Him. I would make Him my example. But my trying to imitate Him will never reproduce His likeness in me.

So, how can I have, actually have, the Spirit of Christ? Only the Spirit of God can produce in us the Spirit of Christ. Unless the unseen power of the Spirit of God is here, the Spirit of Christ will not be here. The unseen Spirit must be here in order for the manifest Spirit to be here. It is the power of the indwelling Spirit of God that transforms the spirits of men until they become in actuality the Spirit of Christ. How do we know that is true? We have the testimony of Scripture.

2 Corinthians 3:3–6 says, *"You show that you are a letter from Christ, the result of our ministry, written not with ink but with the Spirit of the living God, not on tablets of stone but on tablets of human hearts. Such confidence we have through Christ before God. Not that we are competent in ourselves to claim anything for ourselves, but our competence comes from God. He has made us competent as ministers of a new covenant — not of the letter but of the Spirit; for the letter kills, but the Spirit gives life."*

In addition *2 Corinthians 3:17–18* says, *"Now the Lord is the Spirit, and where the Spirit of the Lord is, there is freedom. And we all, who with unveiled faces contemplate the Lord's glory, are being transformed into his image with ever-increasing glory, which comes from the Lord, who is the Spirit."*

We have all witnessed the truth of this, both in our own lives and in the lives of others. Recently I attended the funeral for a man who was our next-door neighbor for almost 40 years. He was a quiet, humble, and unassuming man.

He lived a simple life. He was very devoted to his wife, to their one child, a son, and to his two grandsons. For many years he worked for the post office. He had a unique ability to fix almost anything, and his job at the post office was to keep the equipment running. He retired 15 years ago, and then he made himself available to everyone in our neighborhood to fix things that were broken. At his funeral, his pastor said that he saw that ability as a God-given gift, and he felt an obligation to make it available to anyone who needed it. I cannot count the times that he got our air conditioner or heating system running. He hooked up my computers for me. He repaired computers for me. Anything that broke at my house, Mac fixed. How we will miss him!

Mac was a man of great sensitivity. As he witnessed yard work becoming more difficult for James, he took it upon himself to take up some of the slack. He would blow the leaves off the front driveway, and almost always he would do it while we were gone. We would return home to that nice surprise! Mac could see the trouble I was having with bad knees, and so after James' heart bypass, he would go out each morning and get our newspaper and put it by the front door. In our neighborhood, the mailboxes are out at the street. Mac would bring our mail to us every day.

He loved Sycamore Creek. It runs at the back of our properties. Hard rains would deposit all kinds of trash alongside the creek. He would be out after every rain to pick it up. He kept the creek in pristine condition.

Dr. and Mrs. Evans lived two houses down from Mac. When they could no longer drive, he took it upon himself to take them to church every Sunday morning. All of these things were done so quietly and so unobtrusively that friends were often unaware of what he was doing for months or even years.

Mac lived a life of serenity as well. When he was diagnosed with pancreatic cancer, he came over to tell us about it. He and James sat out in James' spur shop for hours that day just talking. We marveled at how calmly he put his business in order. He sold his house to his nephew, and he and his wife bought a house next door to their son. The chemotherapy worked for a while. We were surprised to see how well he looked and how active he remained. Then it became harder for him to tolerate. He made the decision to discontinue treatment. With calmness and great dignity Mac and his wife faced the inevitable. He wanted it to be known that he had accepted Jesus as his Savior when he was 13. It occurred to me at his funeral that I have never known a man who exhibited the character of Christ any more clearly than Mac did. He did not talk the talk. He walked the walk.

As we draw this lesson to a close, may we remember that our own spirit is a matter of supreme importance. Our spirit is the deepest part of our inner being. It is the center of our God-consciousness. It is the cradle of our character.

What is your character? What is your disposition? What is your nature? The wonderful news is that the powerful Spirit of God can transform it. You can be filled with the Spirit of Christ. Then you will show forth His praises until He comes! *"But you are a chosen people, a royal priesthood, a holy nation, God's special possession, that you may declare the praises of him who called you out of darkness into his wonderful light."* 1 Peter 2:9.

It is important what we believe, but it is important only as belief translates into action. A creed that does not blossom into a gracious character is not worth anything! It is the spirit that matters. All too often, we try to correct the center of our lives from the circumference. We try to fix our lives from the outside in. Rather, may we make corrections from the center out. We do that by handing over to God all that we are. Then we receive into our spirits the Spirit of God, and He is enthroned there. We will no longer be controlled by our flesh. We will live lives that are rooted and grounded in love by the power of the Spirit of God.

All is not accomplished at once. Christian character becomes ours through the process of growth — first the blade, then the ear, then the full corn in the ear. *Mark 4:26–29* reveals this process:

> He also said, "This is what the kingdom
> of God is like. A man scatters seed on the
> ground. Night and day, whether he sleeps or
> gets up, the seed sprouts and grows, though he
> does not know how. All by itself the soil

45

produces grain — first the stalk, then the head, then the full kernel in the head. As soon as the grain is ripe, he puts the sickle to it, because the harvest has come."

It is the Spirit of God in us that brings the promise of the Spirit of Christ being lived out through us, and we "grow up in all things into him who is the Head". Ephesians 4:15. We will read Ephesians 4:11–16 and take special note of verse 13:

"So Christ himself gave the apostles, the prophets, the evangelists, the pastors and teachers, to equip his people for works of service, so that the body of Christ may be built up until we all reach unity in the faith and in the knowledge of the Son of God and become mature, attaining to the whole measure of the fullness of Christ.

Then we will no longer be infants, tossed back and forth by the waves, and blown here and there by every wind of teaching and by the cunning and craftiness of people in their deceitful scheming. Instead, speaking the truth in love, we will grow to become in every respect the mature body of him who is the head, that is, Christ. From him the whole body, joined and held together by every supporting ligament, grows and builds itself up in love, as each part does its work."

I urge you to come to this judgment seat alone. May we each inquire of ourselves as to whether or not our spirit is alive to the Spirit of God. Have we given Him first place in our hearts? Is the Spirit of Christ being revealed through us? If not, we now know the reason. Either we have not received the Spirit of God with the Power and Light and Life that He brings, or we have quenched or resisted or ignored or grieved the Spirit of God that lives in us.

The Bible calls such people "carnal Christians". We find a description of such people in *1 Corinthians 3:1-3.* *"Brothers and sisters, I could not address you as people who live by the Spirit but as people who are still worldly — mere infants in Christ. I gave you milk, not solid food, for you were not yet ready for it. Indeed, you are still not ready. You are still worldly. For since there is jealousy and quarreling among you, are you not worldly? Are you not acting like mere humans?"*

May we not only welcome the Spirit of God, but may we also crown Him Lord of our lives. As our lives demonstrate the Spirit of Christ, may we fulfill God's purpose for us in becoming day by day more like Jesus.

I will close with the words of a song. May it be our closing prayer.

Renewal

Renew me, Father, day by day,
In all my words, in all my ways;
That I'll be more like You, I pray,
Day by day, Lord; day by day.

May love be mine to give away,
To all I meet throughout this day;
That I'll be more like You, I pray;
Day by day, Lord; day by day.

Give strength, my Father, this I pray,
To walk in Your ways all my days;
That I'll be more like You, I pray;
Day by day, Lord; day by day.

When days are gone, when life has passed,
When heaven opens, home at last!
Be this my cry of joy and praise,
More like You, Lord; day by day.

Think On These Things

What is the result of the Spirit of Christ in us? What is the significance of the expression, "the Spirit of God?" Explain your understanding of these two similar expressions as they are presented in this lesson.

What was the secret of the beauty and glory of the life of Jesus? Explain how this provides a daily key for your life.

How does your life reveal your character? Explain why it is not always revealed through the things that you do or the words that you say.

What three words were given here that characterized the life of Jesus? Can you see those three characteristics mirrored in your own life? Give examples. Discuss how they challenge you.

In what ways and at what times are these qualities tested? In what ways are these tests for your benefit? What does it mean that you do what you are?

Describe a recent character test. How did you handle it?

Explain your understanding of what it means that only the Spirit of God can transform your spirit so that it actually becomes the Spirit of Christ. Do you really believe that is possible?

We have read *Romans 8:1–17* several times. It is interesting to note that up to this point in the book of Romans, the Holy Spirit has only been mentioned once. That is in *Romans 5:5. "And hope does not put us to shame, because God's love has been poured out into our hearts through the Holy Spirit, who has been given to us."* In *Romans 8* He is mentioned 19 times. You may want to underline these references in your Bible.

Lesson Three
The Day Of Pentecost: Tongues Like Fire

TEXT: *"And there appeared unto them tongues parting asunder, like as of fire; and it sat upon each one of them."*

Acts 2:3, KJV

This is a familiar verse of Scripture, and perhaps most often we have read it much as we would read an article in the newspaper. It reports an event; and all too often we have not thought further to question the meaning of the event to each of us individually or to the whole wide world.

Forty-nine days had passed since Passover. Men from every nation under heaven had come to Jerusalem to celebrate this Feast of Weeks. Tucked away in an upper room a few people who were insignificant by the world's standards, yet chosen by God to witness the advent of a new world movement, waited.

Their Teacher and Master had been crucified at Passover. With His crucifixion, their hopes that He would set up His kingdom had been shattered. Their love for Him had not faltered, but when their Shepherd was taken the sheep had scattered. Then came the astounding wonder of the resurrection, and that was what had gathered them together again. It had revealed Jesus to be far more than they could ever have imagined!

In a deeper and more profound sense than they had understood before, they now realized that, in truth, Jesus was the Son of God! As Peter expressed it in one of his later letters, they were *"brought again to a living hope through the resurrection of Jesus Christ from the dead."* 1 Peter 1:3. Faith had faltered. Hope had died. Love had lived on. Now, in the light of the resurrection all things had become new.

Jesus had been with them for 40 days. They were strange days, mystical days. Sometimes He would not be with them, and then suddenly He would be there. He would be right there where they were sure He was not! Other times, He would be walking and talking with them or sitting with them at the table; and suddenly He would not be there, right where they were sure He was! These were the strange comings and goings of those 40 days. They were marked by His appearances and disappearances. Through His appearances, they were reassured that He was alive. Through His disappearances they were being trained to do without His physical presence. Then He vanished, and for 10 days they had been waiting in the upper room; waiting for they knew not what!

In that same room Jesus Himself had said to them, *"It is best for you that I go away, for if I do not go away the Comforter will not come to you; but if I go I will send Him to you. When He, the Spirit of truth, is come, He will guide you into all the truth." John 16:13.* Well, what did that mean? What would that be like? They had no idea. Now that promise was about to be fulfilled. The era of the Spirit of God in human history was about to begin! The Christian Church of God was about to be born.

In those initial hours, signs were given. Throughout the history of the Christian Church there have been eras when signs were given, but Dr. Morgan points out that such eras were always preceded by failure. On its highest level, faith does not ask for signs. It does not need them. Signs reach out to those who are spiritually dull and draw them into a new awareness of spiritual things. God, in infinite patience and with amazing grace, gave to these men and women these earliest of signs.

The signs drew attention to new facts, and symbolized them. All of the signs were sensual. There was the sound as of a *"mighty rushing wind"*. There was the sight of the tongues of fire. There was the personal experience of the wondrous gift of tongues. There is not a sentence or phrase here that is not worthy of the closest study, but we are going to focus in this lesson on the one visible sign that was given in that hour; *"Tongues parting asunder, like as of fire." Acts 2:3 KJV.*

This marked the birth of the Christian church. This was the moment when individual men and women were baptized by the Holy Spirit into unity. No longer were they individuals who had come together because of a shared ideal or ethic. No longer were they separate units congregating around a great teacher or leader. They had become a holy company of men and women who were brought into Oneness through all being baptized by the Holy Spirit of God into a living relationship with Jesus Christ. They became part of the body of Christ! *Romans 12:3–5* reveals this:

> *"For by the grace given me I say to every one of you: Do not think of yourself more highly than ought, but rather think of yourself with sober judgment, in accordance with the faith God has distributed to each of you. For just as each of us has one body with many members, and these members do not all have the same function, so in Christ we, though many, form one body, and each member belongs to all the others."*

The initial baptism by the Holy Spirit took place in that upper room, and these people became the body of Christ and the Church of God. With that baptism, they saw tongues parting asunder, as of fire. By that token, God gave to us for all time the true symbol of the Christian church.

Dr. Morgan wrote of the incalculable loss which the church sustained when it forgot this fact and arbitrarily selected other symbols to represent her nature and mission. It may surprise us to hear that the cross is not the symbol of the Christian church, because for generations we have made it our symbol. It appears on our buildings. We incorporate it into our art. We wear it as a sign, and we most often are ignorant of the fact that Almighty God gave us tongues of fire as the true symbol of His church.

Why this insistence that the cross is not the symbol? Why is that important? What difference does it make to us? What does it mean to me? It is crucial to understand because the cross was not the final thing. It was absolutely necessary, but there is much more to the story. A truer symbol than the cross would be an empty grave with the stone rolled away; but even that was not the final thing. The symbol that suggests the nature and the mission of the church is tongues of fire. We should note that in 1968, the United Methodist Church adopted an emblem that incorporates the cross and dual tongues of fire.

First, let us consider the symbolism of the tongue apart from the fire. Human beings are unique in their ability to express thoughts through language. That ability has shaped and defined the course of human history.

The tongue has a power all its own. There is a rich history of men and women, teachers and preachers, politicians and philosophers, who have influenced multitudes and turned the course of events through their ability to persuade. The power of a person who is a strong thinker, who has vigorous convictions, and who can communicate them so as to convince others can scarcely be estimated.

The strength of the tongue is one of the greatest tools we have. God has used that power in a mighty way in the spreading of the Gospel. Think of the power of our personal speech. Through speech we express our thoughts, and argue our positions, and declare our beliefs. There is no other force like it!

The Church's mission in the world is to make Jesus known, and that mission is being carried out through the use of the tongue. The mission is three-fold. The tongue of praise sets forth God's grace and glory. The tongue of prayer speaks to the Father in intercession. The tongue of proclamation declares God's message and reveals His will.

On that day at that moment in that upper room, the Holy Spirit came; and by His coming, He created in history a new institute of praise and of prayer and of proclamation. It flowed out of the reality of men and women who were baptized into a living union with Jesus. They felt the thrill of it, and they were compelled to speak out. The symbol of their new office was that of tongues as of fire and parting asunder, and it sat on each one of them!

On that day the Church of God became the mouthpiece through which praise is articulated. On that day, the Church of God became the mouthpiece through which pastors and the entire priesthood of believers could go before God in prayer with the burdens of suffering humanity. On that day, the Church of God became the mouthpiece of proclamation bringing to all mankind the good news of God's love and of His redemptive mercy. Note carefully that, whether in praise or prayer or proclamation, the instrument is the tongue. The purpose of the existence of the Church on this earth is represented by this symbol. The Church is to speak! That is its business, and it is not the exclusive business of its teachers and preachers.

It is the business of every single individual that shares the Life of Jesus and thereby knows the thrill of His Spirit living in them. Such people want to talk about Him! By the baptism of the Holy Spirit our tongues are fired to proclaim God's goodness to the world. The tongue stands as the symbol and as the reminder that we are to be God's witnesses.

Behind the witness of our tongues must lie the witness of our lives. Do we often talk of the Lord? I think if you begin to speak of Him, you will be surprised how many people are eager to hear of Him. All of us will not have the opportunity to talk to vast audiences, but every one of us will have the opportunity to talk to individuals. Now let us go back to our symbol, and we notice that it is that of a tongue *"like as of fire"*.

What meaning does that hold? Reaching for the depths of meaning we will turn to *Isaiah 6:1-7*. It was the early part of young Isaiah's ministry. For the first time in his life, the throne of Judah was vacant. Taking pen in hand he wrote:

> *"In the year that King Uzziah died, I saw the Lord, high and exalted, seated on a throne; and the train of his robe filled the temple. Above him were seraphim, each with six wings: with two wings they covered their faces, with two they covered their feet, and with two they were flying. And they were calling to one another:*
>
> *'Holy, holy, holy is the LORD Almighty; the whole earth is full of his glory.'*
> *At the sound of their voices the doorposts and thresholds shook and the temple was filled with smoke.*
>
> *'Woe to me!' I cried. 'I am ruined! For I am a man of unclean lips, and I live among a people of unclean lips, and my eyes have seen the King, the LORD Almighty.'*
>
> *Then one of the seraphim flew to me with a live coal in his hand, which he had taken with tongs from the altar. With it he touched my mouth and said, 'See, this has*

touched your lips; your guilt is taken away and your sin atoned for.'"

What is the symbolism of the fire? It does not symbolize inspiration or energy or the end of one thing and the beginning of another, but cleansing. The seraphim touched Isaiah's lips in order to cleanse them. Tongues of fire. Tongues of fire! The fire is that which cleanses the tongue. By way of contrast, let's turn to James and read *James 3:1–12:*

> *"Not many of you should become teachers, my fellow believers; because you know that we who teach will be judged more strictly. We all stumble in many ways. Anyone who is never at fault in what they say is perfect, able to keep their whole body in check.*

> *When we put bits into the mouths of horses to make them obey us, we can turn the whole animal. Or take ships as an example. Although they are so large and are driven by strong winds, they are steered by a very small rudder wherever the pilot wants to go. Likewise, the tongue is a small part of the body, but it makes great boasts. Consider what a great forest is set on fire by a small spark. The tongue also is a fire, a world of evil among the parts of the body. It corrupts the whole body, sets the whole course of one's life on fire, and is itself set on fire by hell.*

> *All kinds of animals, birds, reptiles and sea creatures are being tamed and have been tamed by mankind, but no human being can tame the tongue. It is a restless evil, full of deadly poison.*

> *With the tongue we praise our Lord and Father, and with it we curse human*

beings, who have been made in God's likeness. Out of the same mouth come praise and cursing. My brothers and sisters, this should not be. Can both fresh water and salt water flow from the same spring? My brothers and sisters, can a fig tree bear olives, or a grapevine bear figs? Neither can a salt spring produce fresh water."

This is a strange contrast. It is a pointed contrast! The tongue speaks out of the fire of heaven or out of the fire of hell. The fire behind our words will always be a force of pollution or a force of purification. That will depend on whether the fire behind it originates in heaven or in hell. When tongues are set on fire by hell, what destruction they leave in their wake! Families are destroyed. Friendships are ruined. Reputations are torn down. Communities are shattered. Nations go to war against one another, and all because of the power of the tongue.

Over and against that stands this symbol: the tongue of Holy fire, the fire of the Holy Spirit. It is a fire that cleanses and purifies, that inspires and energizes, that is an influence for all that is high and noble and holy. What comfort it brings! What breaches it heals! What fellowship it creates! Our tongues are to be tongues of fire, but they are to be tongues of Holy fire.

Recently Tom and Linda Wilson returned from their second trip to Rwanda. While they were there they visited the Sonrise School. It was established to take in children that had been affected or orphaned by the genocide experienced there, and to offer them a quality education.

The visiting group was invited to attend a morning chapel session. The speaker was one of the school's own teachers, and the visitors were appalled by her presentation. Although they did not understand her language, her grim face struck them as well as her solemn, forcefully delivered words. For almost an hour her diatribe went on, and finally the elementary grades were dismissed.

Next, the high school students filed in; and Linda was to be their speaker. The words of Jim Rayburn, who founded Young Life, echoed in her ears. "It is a sin to bore young people with the glorious message of Jesus!" She spoke for only 15 minutes. She acknowledged that they had seen terrible things, but she told them that God loves them very much, and that He has a great plan for every one of their lives. She told them that they are beautiful poems that are being written by God. Then she had them all stand, and she led them in a cheer, complete with motions. "We are poems being written by God!"

Throughout the rest of their visit when she encountered a student who had been in chapel that day, a big smile would cover their face, and they would call out that cheer. She was asked to come back again soon because, "You are filled with the light and the life of Jesus, and our children need to experience that!" Such is the reality of *"Tongues as of Fire"*.

This brings us to our last thought. What does the symbol teach us of the interrelationship that needs to exist between the tongue and the fire? The tongue is human. The fire is Divine. The tongue of Fire is the human instrument that is energized and inspired by the Divine Nature. It is a demonstration of the union that exists between God and man for the very purpose of praising, of praying, and of proclaiming the salvation of God.

Praise and prayer and proclamation can be spoken to no avail at all, for it needs the tongue of Fire to say it. It is human speech united with Divine power that reveals and cleanses and persuades and empowers.

Don't miss the phrase that is used here. Tongues, (plural) *"like as of fire; and it"*, (singular) *"sat upon each of them"*. It was one fire parting into tongues, "and it sat upon each one of them." This is not a statement that on each head there was a tongue of fire. It is a statement that upon each head sat a tongue of that which was One Fire. Behind the tongues stood One Spirit. On whom did this symbol rest? It rested upon men and women alike.

Reading on, we see that Peter referred to a quotation from Joel that was fulfilled through this experience.

> *Then Peter stood up with the eleven, raised his voice and addressed the crowd; "Fellow Jews and all of you who live in Jerusalem, let me explain this to you; listen carefully to what I say. These men are not drunk, as you suppose. It's only nine in the morning! No, this is what was spoken by the prophet Joel:*
>
> *'In the last days, God says, I will pour out my Spirit on all people. Your sons and daughters will prophesy, your old men will dream dreams, Even on my servants, both men and women, I will pour out my Spirit in those days, and they will prophesy.'"*
>
> *Acts 2:14–18.*

"Your old men shall dream dreams." Dreams often have to do with the past. The words here are that the old men will speak of the past in ways that enable those of a new generation to understand it. *"Your young men shall see visions."* Visions most often have to do with the future. Young men will speak of the future with words of promise and hope. Such is the message of tongues anointed with Holy Fire.

So what is the great message of truth that this symbolism speaks of? It tells us that the Church of God, established on that day, is God's instrument of declaration and of witness. Every single member is responsible for proclaiming and witnessing in the power of the Holy Spirit.

Our weakness is absolute. In our own strength and by our own effort, our praise, our prayers, and our proclamation will amount to nothing at all. As born-again children of God, we are anointed with the Holy Spirit of God. As surely as He lives, He is living in us! Pentecost is operational today. Spiritual power is ours today. This is what it means to be a Christian.

We do not often receive visible signs, but we do have the promise of Jesus that His presence and His power are always with us. He is here, our Paraclete, our Advocate, our Comforter, our Teacher, and our Guide. He comes and cleanses our tongues with the fire of God in order that, through them, He will win victories and establish His kingdom in our lives, in our homes, in our churches and communities, and out into the whole wide world.

God, We Adore You

God above the heavens, we adore You.
Spirit of our God, we give You praise.
Jesus, Son of God, we pledge our honor and our love.
To God the Three-in-One, our voices raise.

We bring You honor, we bring You glory.
You call us by Your Name.
We bring You honor, we bring all glory
To our God, who will forever reign!

God above the heavens, we adore You.
Spirit of our God, we give You praise.
Jesus, Son of God, we pledge our honor and our love.
To God the Three-in-One, our voices raise.

Think On These Things

Could Christianity have survived without the coming of the Holy Spirit? Explain your answer.

What meaning does His coming have for you as you go about living a Christian life?

Write down some of your thoughts about the power of your tongue. Give one example of how that power played out in your life this week.

In our lesson, we considered a "three-fold mission" for the tongue: praise, prayer, and proclamation. Write about what place these things hold in your life. How are they incorporated into who you are? What does your life and the words you speak bear witness to?

"The fire behind our words will always be a force of pollution or of purification." What does that mean? Give an example from your experience.

I think you will enjoy reading and thinking about 1 Corinthians 12:4–31.

Lesson Four
The Holy Spirit Has Come

TEXT: *"Exalted to the right hand of God, he (Jesus Christ) has received from the Father the promised Holy Spirit, and has poured out what you now see and hear."*

Acts 2:33, NIV

There are two historic facts concerning Christianity that cannot be disputed: the death of Jesus and the Church of Jesus. History records the fact that after the death of Jesus, new energy and power swept through human history. A new order of men and women emerged with new ideals, new determination, and with new force that led to a new order in society — the Church of Jesus Christ!

In the book of Acts we read the story of the beginning of the Christian movement; and in *Acts 2* we find the first burst of light and power that followed the resurrection and ascension of Jesus. The disciples were gathered together once again in the upper room. They are there to mark the Feast of Pentecost. Without warning, they heard a sound like a gale force wind filling the building. They saw what seemed to be tongues of fire that separated and came to rest on each of them. They began to speak in different languages. Read *Acts 2:1–13* and allow yourself to be caught up in the fascination, the thrill, and the power of it!

> *"When the day of Pentecost came, they were all together in one place. Suddenly a sound like the blowing of a violent wind came from heaven and filled the whole house where they were sitting. They saw what seemed to be tongues of fire that separated*

and came to rest on each of them. All of them were filled with the Holy Spirit and began to speak in other tongues as the Spirit enabled them.

Now there were staying in Jerusalem God-fearing Jews from every nation under heaven. When they heard this sound, a crowd came together in bewilderment, because each one heard their own language being spoken. Utterly amazed, they asked: 'Aren't all these who are speaking Galileans? Then how is it that each of us hears them in our native language? Parthians, Medes and Elamites; residents of Mesopotamia, Judea and Cappadocia, Pontus and Asia, Phrygia and Pamphylia, Egypt and the parts of Libya near Cyrene; visitors from Rome (both Jews and converts to Judaism); Cretans and Arabs — we hear them declaring the wonders of God in our own tongues!' Amazed and perplexed, they asked one another, 'What does this mean?'

Some, however, made fun of them and said, 'They have had too much wine.'"

The coming of the Holy Spirit that began at Pentecost abides today. You may have heard people pray for a new Pentecost, but there will never be another one. On Pentecost, the Spirit of God came with the purpose of creating and abiding with the Church of God forever, and He has never withdrawn. He is here with us today in this place. His presence and power is here, just as surely as He was in that upper room in Jerusalem. The Spirit proceeds from the Father through the Son and into the lives of all who believe on Him. We may not hear the sound of a rushing wind. We may not see the tongues of fire, but that very same Spirit is being poured out on us and on all who believe in the Lord Jesus Christ.

With that said, we might well ask about the cause of the failure we see in the church of Jesus Christ and in the lives of individual Christians. We might ask, "Why don't we experience the same thing?"

There were experiences that day that were not meant to abide. They were necessary for that time; and although the experience passed, the truths have not passed. We don't ask for the signs — the sound of rushing wind and the appearance of tongues of fire — but we do ask for the power. We long to know the experience that brought ecstasy and joy and song. What secrets moved men to proclaim the good news and to live transformed lives of total obedience to Christ?

We have already said that the tongue of fire was the first symbol of the Christian church. The outpouring of the Spirit brought joy and fullness of life. This was expressed when men praised God in different tongues. The Holy Spirit was given first and foremost in order for men to offer praise to God. It was a gift that enabled praise! The disciples were declaring the wonders of God.

We discover here that praise and thanksgiving is the first function of the Christian church. Have we understood that? It is the first and most important function of the priesthood of believers. The coming of the Spirit of Life opened the eyes of these disciples, and they were able to see as they had never seen before. They were able to understand things they had never understood before — things concerning Jesus and things concerning the Father. The Holy Spirit brought to the disciples fullness of life, and out of that came fullness of joy, and out of that came words that honored and glorified the name of God and which sounded His praises abroad. The multitudes heard them in their own languages bearing witness to the mighty works of God!

What was the result? Jerusalem was brought to a stop! The people of that city had no explanation for what was happening. They searched for an explanation, but they could not find one. It was not a preacher that brought the city to a halt. It was a Spirit-filled church. Their joy, their praise, and their ecstasy demonstrated the fullness of Life that they were experiencing. That set the stage for the preacher to declare the good news of the gospel, and that is exactly what Peter did. The message of Peter that we find here, is the first word that was given to men outside of the small group of disciples through the power of the Spirit. Watch carefully as it all unfolds. We are going to read *Acts 2:14-21*.

> *Then Peter stood up with the Eleven, raised his voice and addressed the crowd: "Fellow Jews and all of you who live in Jerusalem, let me explain this to you; listen carefully to what I say. These people are not drunk, as you suppose. It's only nine in the morning! No, this is what was spoken by the prophet Joel:*
>
> *'In the last days, God says, I will pour out my Spirit on all people. Your sons and daughters will prophesy, your young men will see visions, your old men will dream dreams. Even on my servants, both men and women, I will pour out my Spirit in those days, and they will prophesy. I will show wonders in the heavens above and signs on the earth below, blood and fire and billows of smoke. The sun will be turned to darkness and the moon to blood before the coming of the great and glorious day of the Lord. And everyone who calls on the name of the Lord will be saved.'"*

Next, Peter clearly connects the event of the Pentecostal baptism to Jesus. After quoting from the prophecy of Joel, after declaring that the signs and circumstances they found themselves in were the fulfillment of prophecy, Peter seized their attention once again when he said, *"Fellow Israelites, listen to this."*

Then, in an orderly sequence he told the story of Jesus of Nazareth. That was his most familiar name by which he had been known. It was the name that His disciples used in love and that other men used in contempt. Peter declared that Jesus' miracles bore witness to his flawless nature. The distinction was carefully made that the miracles and the wondrous things that Jesus did were all works of God that were accomplished through the perfection of his humanity. Listen to the words of Peter. We pick up here at *Acts 2:22.*

"Jesus of Nazareth was a man accredited by God to you by miracles, wonders and signs, which God did among you through him, as you yourselves know." Then Peter came to the last fact: *"This man was handed over to you by God's deliberate plan and foreknowledge; and you, with the help of wicked men, put him to death by nailing him to the cross."*

These words pulled together all that these men knew of Jesus. Here were the things they had seen with their own eyes. Here was Jesus of Nazareth, a man who had been revealed to them by God through great signs and wonders. He was a man who had been crucified. Their knowledge could not take them beyond this. They thought the cross had ended his story.

However, Peter had much more to say! In *Acts 2:24-36* he told them of the events that followed the cross. *"But God raised him from the dead, freeing him from the agony of death, because it was impossible for death to keep its hold on him."*

David said about him: "I saw the Lord always before me. Because he is at my right hand, I will not be shaken. Therefore my heart is glad and my tongue rejoices; my body will also rest in hope, because you will not abandon me to the realm of the dead, you will not let your holy one see decay. You have made known to me the paths of life; you will fill me with joy in your presence."

"Fellow Israelites, I can tell you confidently that the patriarch David died and was buried and his tomb is here to this day. But he was a prophet and knew that God had promised him on oath that he would place one of his descendants on his throne. Seeing what was to come, he spoke of the resurrection of the Messiah, that he was not abandoned to the realm of the dead, nor did his body see decay. God has raised this Jesus to life, and we are all witnesses of it. Exalted to the right hand of God, he has received from the Father the promised Holy Spirit and has poured out what you now see and hear. Therefore let all Israel be assured of this: God has made this Jesus, whom you crucified, both Lord and Messiah."

In these words Peter explained to them the fullness of life that had expressed itself in the praises that had amazed the city. How did the people respond? *"When the people heard this, they were cut to the heart and said to Peter and the other apostles, 'Brothers, what shall we do?' Peter replied, 'Repent and be baptized, every one of you, in the name of Jesus Christ for the forgiveness of your sins. And you will receive the gift of the Holy Spirit. The promise is for you and your children and for all who are far off — for all whom the Lord our God will call.'*

With many other words he warned them; and he pleaded with them. 'Save yourselves from this corrupt generation.' Those who accepted his message were baptized, and about three thousand were added to their number that day." Acts 2:37-41.

Now notice carefully the conflict between grace and sin. Here we will see the Love of God revealed through Divine activity and the hostility toward God revealed through human activity. The entire course of Jesus' ministry is revealed in this wonderful paragraph, and we see Him clearly as the center of perpetual conflict between God's grace on the one hand and sin on the other. Observe the movement of sin. It first expressed itself as blindness when confronted with the revelation of the life of Jesus. Jesus' words and His works witnessed to the truth of His Life, but many who saw Him and heard Him did not understand. Although they had eyes, they did not see. Although they had ears, they did not hear.

They closed their eyes. They hardened their hearts, and their sin was fully expressed when Jesus was nailed to the cross. There they refuted His teachings. They refused His Kingship. They rejected His moral requirements and His offer of pardon and forgiveness and grace. Sin had done its worst. The Lord of glory lay dead. It was simply rude superstition that ordered a watch over His grave.

We stand as witnesses of this same process today. How many of those we know and love are blind to the revelation of God concerning Jesus? How many witness the Light and Life He gives to others, but fail to understand His offer to them of a New Life? Just as with men of old, they close their eyes and harden their hearts. They reject His teachings, refuse His Kingship, and mock His moral requirements. They crucify Him anew. Thus we see the movement of sin.

Now watch the activity of grace. Jesus' life had revealed God and His will concerning mankind. Jesus was calling us back to Himself! And what of the cross? Did sin win a victory there? Was grace defeated? Was God's purpose frustrated? Let us go back to that parenthesis, *"handed over to you by God's set purpose and foreknowledge"*. Acts 2:23.

No one saw the cross in that light until after Pentecost. It became clear to the disciples as they saw it in the light of the resurrection. It was through looking back in the light of the Spirit that Peter and the others saw God at work at the cross. They could see the decisiveness of His love. They could see something of the mystery of His authority and power over sin. They could see that He had dealt with it and had emerged victorious over it. Thus we see the activity of grace.

Let us look at the next step that Peter suggested in his address. The victory had been won. The Lord had been raised from the dead, and He had been raised in dignity and with power and glory. That was followed by His bodily ascent into heaven.

Through Peter's address we are able to follow Jesus of Nazareth into the blinding light, the radiance, and the glory of heaven. Through Peter, listen to the Holy Spirit speak of what took place in that sacred hour. *"The Lord Jesus Christ received from the Father the promised Holy Spirit."* *Acts 2: 33.* In *John 14:16-17* we read that, before His crucifixion, Jesus said to His disciples, *"I will ask the Father, and He will give you another Counselor to be with you forever, even the Spirit of Truth. The world cannot accept Him because it neither sees Him nor knows Him, but you know Him, for He lives with you and will be in you."*

Also consider *John 14: 25–27.* *" All this I have spoken while still with you. But the Advocate, the Holy Spirit, whom the Father will send in my name, will teach you all things and will remind you of everything I have said to you. Peace I leave with you; my peace I give you. I do not give to you as the world gives. Do not let your hearts be troubled and do not be afraid."* In addition, see *John 15:26: "When the Advocate comes, whom I will send to you from the Father — the Spirit of truth who goes out from the Father — he will testify about me."*

We can only understand as we realize that Jesus passed into that heavenly place as the representative one. He passed in as our representative. He was representing us! That was the moment man returned to God, and God returned to man in Christ. He asked, as He had said He would, for the gift of the Holy Spirit in order that He might bestow it on all who trusted in Him.

Now we see Jesus in the presence of God, the risen Man and the ascended Lord. He stands there in the place of those He left behind. He was wounded for them. He was bruised for them. He had taken their place on the cross. In *Isaiah 53: 3–12*, we read:

> *"He was despised and rejected by mankind, a man of suffering, and familiar with pain. Like one from whom people hide their faces he was despised, and we held him in low esteem.*
>
> *Surely he took up our pain and bore our suffering, yet we considered him punished by God, stricken by him, and afflicted. But he was pierced for our transgressions, he was crushed for our iniquities; the punishment that brought us peace was on him, and by his wounds we are healed. We all, like sheep, have gone astray, each of us has turned to our own way; and the LORD has laid on him the iniquity of us all.*
>
> *He was oppressed and afflicted, yet he did not open his mouth; he was led like a lamb to the slaughter, and as a sheep before its shearers is silent, so he did not open his mouth. By oppression and judgment he was taken away. Yet who of his generation protested? For he was cut off from the land of the living; for the transgression of my people he was punished. He was assigned a grave with the wicked and with the rich in his death, though he had done no violence, nor was any deceit in his mouth.*
>
> *Yet it was the LORD's will to crush him and cause him to suffer, and though the LORD makes his life an offering for sin, he will see his offspring and prolong his days, and the will of the LORD will prosper in his hand. After he has suffered, he will see the light of*

life and be satisfied; by his knowledge my righteous servant will justify many, and he will bear their iniquities. Therefore I will give him a portion among the great, and he will divide the spoils with the strong, because he poured out his life unto death, and was numbered with the transgressors. For he bore the sin of many, and made intercession for the transgressors."

He had overcome their sin. Now He receives the Holy Spirit for them. It was not all for them alone, but for us as well who believe on Him through their word. *John 17:20–26* reveals this:

"My prayer is not for them alone. I pray also for those who will believe in me through their message, that all of them may be one, Father, just as you are in me and I am in you. May they also be in us so that the world may believe that you have sent me. I have given them the glory that you gave me, that they may be one as we are one — I in them and you in me — so that they may be brought to complete unity. Then the world will know that you sent me and have loved them even as you have loved me.

Father, I want those you have given me to be with me where I am, and to see my glory, the glory you have given me because you loved me before the creation of the world.

Righteous Father, though the world does not know you, I know you, and they know that you have sent me. I have made you known to them, and will continue to make you known in order that the love you have for me may be in them and that I myself may be in them."

And so we see that, on the Day of Pentecost, the Holy Spirit came to these men in answer to the prayer of Jesus. The Spirit did not come in answer to their prayers. He didn't come in response to their obedience. He came absolutely and entirely in answer to a prayer that was prayed in heavenly places by Jesus Christ Himself. The Spirit was given by the Father through the Son. Those on whom the Spirit fell were united to the Son.

That is how He comes to us today. We do not receive the Spirit in answer to our prayers. We don't receive the Spirit as a reward for sacrifices we make. Prayer and sacrifice stand as evidence that the Holy Spirit has come to us. However, the coming of the Holy Spirit to make us one with the Lord, His coming to live within us so that the Spirit of Christ dominates us, His coming to express power through our lives — all this and more is in answer to the prayer of Jesus. It comes to us as the result of all that He has done on our behalf.

What was the value of the baptism of Pentecost to the world? It was the creation of the Christian Church of God. This was an entirely new thing, a completely new reality, a new nation, and a new people. Up until that moment, these men had been individual Disciples of Christ. Then they were brought into living union with the Lord Himself. They were brought into living union with each other; and the Christian Church of God was born.

What is its purpose in the world today? Is its number-one purpose evangelism? Is its number-one purpose to teach and inform? Is its number-one purpose fellowship? Is its number one purpose social justice? What does the Bible say?

In *1 Peter 2:9* we read, *"But you are a chosen people, a royal priesthood, a holy nation, a people belonging to God, that you may declare the praises of him who called you out of darkness into his wonderful light."* The whole church was created first of all to praise God!

The church was created to be what Dr. Morgan called "God's institute of praise!" Its first function is that of praise. The Christian church exists to reveal God, to make Him known to all who do not know Him. As they stand before that amazing revelation, it will fill them with wonder and awe and praise.

The world can only know God as He is revealed through His people. The Word of God is powerful only as we live it out. The message of Pentecost is that there is no more important way to live it out than through praise and thanksgiving.

When Jesus was born in Bethlehem, God did not move closer to humanity, but He became visible. As the life of Jesus is reproduced through us, He becomes visible today. He becomes visible through us, and our first business is that of praising Him! Our lips should praise Him. Our songs should praise Him. Our lives should praise Him. Our habits should praise Him. Our ways should stand in perpetual testimony of His being and of the fact of His love. We should be people who live to the praise of His glory! Read here *Ephesians 1:3–14:*

"Praise be to the God and Father of our Lord Jesus Christ, who has blessed us in the heavenly realms with every spiritual blessing in Christ. For he chose us in him before the creation of the world to be holy and blameless in his sight.

In love he predestined us for adoption to sonship through Jesus Christ, in accordance with his pleasure and will — to the praise of his glorious grace, which he has freely given us in the One he loves. In him we have redemption through his blood, the forgiveness of sins, in accordance with the riches of God's grace that he lavished on us. With all wisdom and understanding, He made known to us the mystery of his will according to his good pleasure, which he purposed in Christ, to be put into effect when the times reach their fulfilment— to bring unity to all things in heaven and on earth under Christ.

In him we were also chosen, having been predestined according to the plan of him who works out everything in conformity with the purpose of his will, in order that we, who were the first to put our hope in Christ, might be for the praise of his glory. And you also were included in Christ when you heard the message of truth, the gospel of your salvation.

When you believed, you were marked in him with a seal, the promised Holy Spirit, who is a deposit guaranteeing our inheritance until the redemption of those who are God's possession — to the praise of His glory."
Ephesians 1:3-14.

This was the first effect that the Church produced. The city saw these people filled with Life and Light. They heard them magnifying God for His mighty works. In that hour and by the coming of the Holy Spirit, God had created for Himself a people for His own praise and glory! He had created a kingdom of priests to offer sacrifices of praise and thanksgiving.

This is what Pentecost should produce in our lives. We will discover that praise and thanksgiving is not something we do for God as much as it is something He does for us. Praise and thanksgiving in all things is evidence of His ongoing work in and through us.

Something else was created in that hour. God created what Dr. Morgan referred to as "an institute of prayer." The function of the priesthood of believers is not only the function of thanksgiving and praise. It is also the function of intercession. With the coming of the Holy Spirit, God created for Himself a people who are able to pray.

The Spirit of God understands our pain individually and collectively. The agony of humanity grieves Him. The Holy Spirit who indwells those of us who are God's own people interprets to us the grief and suffering of others. We are brought into an experience of compassionate sympathy with them, and in the very midst of it, we make up an institute of prayer.

All of us live in the midst of the agony of this world. It is only as the Holy Spirit interprets that agony for us that we are able to pray rightly. He leads us into the deepest meaning of its pain, and we no longer see it as something that can be dealt with from the outside in. We come to realize that problems reside in the hearts of mankind. Out of that understanding, created in the hearts of believers by the Spirit of Christ, we are able to pray for healing from the inside out.

As we saw in our last lesson, it was not for praise alone that the Church was created. It was not for prayer alone, but also for proclamation. The church stands today as God's institute of proclamation. Our words and our lives should not only praise God and pray to Him. Our words and our lives should proclaim Him.

The Holy Spirit made the risen and ascended Christ a bright reality to those early disciples. In doing that, He made it possible for them to speak of Him as those who knew Him well. In the things they did, in the words they spoke, in the tone of their voices, in their daily habits, their lives revealed the Lord. Just by being with them, people experienced Jesus!

When the Holy Spirit came, He united all of the believers in Christ. The Spirit multiplied the praise, the prayers, and the proclamation of Jesus throughout the world, showing forth the glory of God in a great demonstration of His power.

As we conclude, may we recognize that our relationship with Jesus determines our possession of the power of Pentecost. Today, in every one of our lives, a conflict still exists; and it is between sin and grace. On which side have we taken our stand? I'm quite certain each one of us would answer, "Why we stand on the side of grace. There's no question about that. Of course, we do!"

But let me state the question in another way. What is the influence of our lives? The answer reveals to us the truth as to whether or not we possess the Spirit of Christ. We have seen that *Romans 8:9* reads, *"If any one does not have the Spirit of Christ, he does not belong to Christ."* Do we have the Spirit of Christ? Is the deepest desire of our hearts to crown Him Lord of our lives and make Him known to others? We can know by this sign that the Spirit of God has been given to us.

However, another question remains. Are we living in all of the fullness and privilege of the Spirit? Does the witness of our lives bring praise and honor to His name? Do we know and experience the secret of prayer that addresses the agony of this world and brings comfort and hope? Do our words and our actions stand as proclamations of the good news of Jesus?

How is all of this translated to be lived out through our lives? I came to believe long ago that the testimony of every life is as totally unique as a fingerprint. There are many stories that could be told to illustrate that truth, but I am going to close this lesson with a story about my Aunt Jettie.

Aunt Jettie was my mother's older sister. For many years she was an elementary school teacher, and for many years she also taught Sunday School classes for children and high school students. When she was in her 40s she met and married Uncle Bill. He was a Presbyterian minister.

They shared a happy life, and when they reached their 70s they moved to a retirement center, Go Ye Village, in Tahlequah, Oklahoma. Shortly after that move Uncle Bill died. Now a widow, Aunt Jettie began looking for something productive with which to fill her days.

At the center they had an extended care facility where long term hospital care was available. Aunt Jettie took that on as her special project. Every day she would head over to the center to visit with the patients. She loved to read, and she would go from room to room reading one chapter per day from books of her choosing. The patients eagerly looked forward to her visits!

Before long my father died, and these two sisters reconnected and began to travel the world. That culminated in their making friends in Hawaii who invited them to spend every winter on their Maui estate. They were having a grand time!

Just days after returning from a Maui visit, Aunt Jettie was rushed to the hospital with internal hemorrhaging. While on the operating table she experienced a stroke that left her unable to talk. Aunt Jettie was always a talker; and there was nothing she loved to talk about more than Jesus and the good news of the gospel. Now she could no longer even ask for a drink of water! However, her mind was clear and alert. When she recovered enough to return to Go Ye Village she wasted no time establishing her daily routine. Every morning she got up early and dressed herself beautifully. After breakfast she would get her walker and head over to the hospital wing.

Now she spent her time with the most critically and chronically ill. She spent her days going from one bed to the other, simply sitting quietly next to the patient and holding their hand or stroking their arm. Often her head would be bowed in silent prayer. Nurses began to notice that people who had not responded to any stimulation for weeks or months began to respond to her presence and to her touch.

Her last two and a half years of life were a demonstration of praise, of prayer, and of proclamation. The proclamation was the testimony of her life itself. Her smile was bright with joy and was totally infectious. Sitting with her in a restaurant one day we had two strangers come by our table to remark that she was the most beautiful woman they had ever seen! It was the shekinah glory of God that shone through her. Her love reached out to include all in its warmth.

There was a man at Go Ye Village who had retired as a minister of the gospel. After Aunt Jettie's death he told us that he came to know Christ as his Savior after observing the radiance and the triumph with which she accepted her limitations. It made him question whether or not he knew the Lord, for he did not believe he could have met that stringent test with the strength and victory she showed. On his knees he accepted the gift of a new birth. What happiness that would have brought to Aunt Jettie!

Right now, may we search our hearts. Have we welcomed the Spirit of God? When we place belief in our living Lord, He comes to take up residence in us. Then, He continues with us. He responds to the degree and attitude of faith that we maintain, flowing in and out, and filling us at times to overflowing! Let us understand that union with Jesus in life and service can only be ours through the presence and the power of the Holy Spirit, and it is a gift of God the Father that comes to us through our Lord and Savior, Jesus Christ.

Spirit Of God, Fall On Me

Spirit of God, fall on me.
Spirit of God, fall on me.
Come fill me, Spirit,
Come set my soul free.
Holy Spirit of God, fall on me.

Jesus, my Savior, come be
More now than life, Lord, to me.
May I know You as my comfort, my guide.
Precious Jesus, my Savior, abide.

Father, One God, show to me
All that You want me to be.
Trusting You ever in ways large and small,
Knowing You as my all in all.
Holy Spirit of God, fall on me.

Think On These Things

What was the first gift that the Holy Spirit brought? What was the purpose of that gift? How does that gift point us to the most important function of the priesthood of believers? Are you living out this law of Pentecost in your life? Explain your answer.

What is the result of lives lived in praise and thanksgiving? Explain how you have seen results played out in your own life or in the life of someone you know.

God demonstrated His approval of Jesus through the wondrous things which were accomplished through His humility and His obedience. They stand as the witness of His life. To what does your life bear witness? What reality stands behind the message of your witness?

How does sin first express itself? Watch its movement from blindness to deafness to hardness of heart. Do you remember a time in your life when that was the expression of your life? Tell what you recall of it.

Seeing the movement of sin, let us reconsider the activity of grace. Grace originated in the foreknowledge and set purpose of God. Jesus passed into heaven as the Representative One and asked His Father to send His Holy Spirit to us. What did you learn from this lesson about how and why the Holy Spirit comes today?

Explain why we are not called to be "Lone Ranger" Christians. Why is fellowship with other Christians critical?

How would you explain proclamation as a law of Pentecost?

How does God equip us to pray? How do prayers contribute to the creation of new things?

In what ways are you living in the fullness and privilege of the Holy Spirit? In what ways would you like to grow to a new level of maturity?

I think you will enjoy reading and thinking about *I John 4:1-13.*

Lesson Five
Filled With The Holy Spirit

TEXT: *"All of them were filled with the Holy Spirit."*

Acts 2:4, NIV

The most important truth about the Day of Pentecost was that the disciples were all filled with the Holy Spirit. The sound of wind and the appearance of tongues of fire were not necessary to the coming of the Holy Spirit, but they were symbolic of His coming.

These people who had received the Holy Spirit were giving praise and thanksgiving to God out of the overflow of gladness in their hearts! The wind, the fire, and the tongues ushered in the coming of the Holy Spirit to all of them. Our text emphasizes the act of His coming. Luke wrote the Book of Acts; and he emphasizes that in that place and at that time and under those conditions this amazing thing took place.

It had been 10 days since these people had last seen Jesus. They had been waiting. There they were — the apostles, with the women and with Jesus' mother and His brothers — waiting in the upper room for they knew not what! What would this promised experience be like? What would this experience hold for them?

Then, quite suddenly, they were all caught up by the Spirit, overpowered by the Spirit, born of the Spirit into a new consciousness of Jesus, and of themselves, and of everything! In a way they could not explain, they found themselves in a closer relationship with Jesus than they had experienced when He had been among them. They began to grasp things He had said that had been mysteries to them. They remembered things He had done that they had not understood. In that very hour they came to a new understanding of Jesus.

They knew now how incomplete had been their perspective of His ministry. Only 10 days earlier they had asked Him if He was now going to restore the Kingdom to Israel. Was He going to establish an earthly kingdom? On this day there dawned upon them a realization of the vastness of His kingdom and the immensity of His mission. Their own hearts were the center of the whole wide world — Jerusalem, Judea, Samaria, and beyond — and they found themselves to be the appointed messengers of this good news!

They also came to a new awareness of themselves. They could suddenly see their own weaknesses. They could recognize their own foolishness. They could see clearly past actions that now saddened them. All became new in that hour: God, and life, and the world!

This small group of people had been walking with Jesus for the past 3 years, but looking back in the light of Pentecost's glory, they saw that it was all far, far greater than anything they could possibly have imagined. They became aware of a power that was transforming them and driving them forward to proclaim the truths of Jesus. Up until that very minute, there had never been a "Christian" in the entire world, apart from Jesus Christ. This was the beginning point of Christianity!

In this lesson, we will consider this experience of Pentecost — first, in relation to the work of Jesus, second, in relation to the experience of the disciples, and third, in relation to our personal experience.

In reference to the work of Jesus, we see Pentecost as the culmination of His earthly ministry and the beginning of his heavenly mission. The Lord Jesus Christ, the Son of God and the Savior of the world, began this work on the day of Pentecost. Everything else He had done had been in preparation for this! Throughout His ministry, throughout His crucifixion and after His resurrection until He ascended to heaven, His earthly experience was one of limitation. He felt it keenly. From the moment that the Holy Spirit came and filled these men, the constraint was gone. Barriers were torn down. Bonds were broken. Christianity began.

Before we move forward, let us quickly review the work of Jesus. In order to do that, we must go into a place that lies beyond and outside our understanding. We will not perfectly grasp what we encounter there, but Scripture draws aside the veil to reveal some unique things about the Son of God in eternity past. Scripture tells us that Christ's ministry did not begin on earth, but in heaven. *Philippians 2: 6-8* takes us to that time and place, and it is here that we read of how Jesus "emptied himself":

"Who, being in very nature God, did not consider equality with God something to be used to his own advantage; rather, he made himself nothing by taking the very nature of a servant, being made in human likeness. And being found in appearance as a man, he humbled himself by becoming obedient to death — even death on a cross!"

We cannot fathom this mystery, but we can say that Jesus laid aside all of His rights as God in the interest of humanity. Jesus is God; fully equal to the Father and to the Holy Spirit. However, He did not hold onto those rights to His own advantage. Rather, He whose form was suitable to heaven agreed to be born of the Spirit and to take on the form of a man, a form suitable to earth. Try to imagine it! He moved from sovereignty to submission. He had always cooperated with the Holy Spirit on an equal basis, but throughout His entire life on earth He consented to be used as an instrument of the Holy Spirit and as the servant of His Father. In doing this, He provided us with an example of our calling.

The first step that the Son of God took in God's plan for human redemption was that of emptying himself. The final step was that of filling men. *"They were all filled with the Holy Spirit."* He had emptied Himself, and now he filled them. He told His disciples that He would ask the Father, and the Father would give Him the Holy Spirit to pour out on them. We read of this in *John 14:1–21*:

> *"Do not let your hearts be troubled. You believe in God; believe also in me. My Father's house has many rooms; if that were not so, would I have told you that I am going there to prepare a place for you? And if I go and prepare a place for you, I will come back and take you to be with me that you also may be where I am. You know the way to the place where I am going."*
>
> *Thomas said to him, "Lord, we don't know where you are going, so how can we know the way?"*
>
> *Jesus answered, "I am the way and the truth and the life. No one comes to the Father except through me. If you really know me, you will know my Father as well. From now on, you do know him and have seen him."*
>
> *Philip said, "Lord, show us the Father and that will be enough for us."*
>
> *Jesus answered, "Don't you know me, Philip, even after I have been among you such a long time? Anyone who has seen me has seen the Father. How can you say, 'Show us the Father?' Don't you believe that I am in the Father, and that the Father is in me? The words I say to you I do not speak on my*

own authority. Rather, it is the Father, living in me, who is doing his work. Believe me when I say that I am in the Father and the Father is in me; or at least believe on the evidence of the works themselves.

Very truly I tell you, whoever believes in me will do the works I have been doing, and they will do even greater things than these, because I am going to the Father. And I will do whatever you ask in my name, so that the Father may be glorified in the Son. You may ask me for anything in my name, and I will do it.

If you love me, keep my commands. And I will ask the Father, and he will give you another advocate to help you and be with you forever — the Spirit of truth. The world cannot accept him, because it neither sees him nor knows him. But you know him, for he lives with you and will be in you.

I will not leave you as orphans; I will come to you. Before long the world will not see me anymore, but you will see me. Because I live, you also will live. On that day you will realize that I am in my Father, and you are in me, and I am in you. Whoever has my commands and obeys them, he is the one who loves me. He who loves me will be loved by my Father, and I too will love him and show myself to him."

That was when a new day arrived in human history. That was the day that new life, a new creation appeared on earth, and that was the day that Christianity was established. Read *2 Corinthians 5:17–21.*

"Therefore, if anyone is in Christ, the new creation has come: The old has gone, the

new is here! All this is from God, who reconciled us to himself through Christ and gave us the ministry of reconciliation: that God was reconciling the world to himself in Christ, not counting people's sins against them. And he has committed to us the message of reconciliation. We are therefore Christ's ambassadors, as though God were making his appeal through us. We implore you on Christ's behalf: Be reconciled to God. God made him who had no sin to be sin for us, so that in him we might become the righteousness of God."

We have seen that the first act that took place leading to our redemption was the emptying of Jesus. The last act was the filling of these people with the Holy Spirit. In between were all those events with which we are so familiar. He was made flesh and He lived among them. He went about teaching and doing good. He bore the sins of mankind to the cross. He broke the power of death when He rose from the dead. He ascended to His Father and asked Him to send the Holy Spirit to be with us. He poured out that gift at Pentecost.

In the New Testament the gift of the Holy Spirit is described as a new birth, a baptism, an anointing, and a sealing. These phrases describe different phases of one great act. To be filled by the Holy Spirit is the most important matter, for the filling includes it all.

The filling of the Spirit is, first of all, a baptism. Baptism suggests death that leads to life. This is fundamental to the Christian experience. We die to ourselves, to our independence, to our self-centeredness, to our self-determined perspectives, and become alive to God. Our dependence is on Him. Our lives are centered on Him. His perspectives become our perspectives. We die to what is false and are raised to what is true. We die to sin and are raised to holiness. We die to a world that is separated from God in order to rise to a life that is eternally one with Him. The receiving of the Holy Spirit is baptism of the Spirit into Life!

All who are baptized by the Spirit of God are baptized into service for Him. Then they are anointed by Him in preparation for their mission. In the Old Testament the priests were anointed for holy service. Their anointing signified that they had been set apart to serve God, and it also signified that their reliance was no longer in themselves. Their effectiveness would be the result of the work of God in them and through them.

Just so, under the New Covenant of the New Testament, all of God's people are anointed for service. *"Now it is God who makes both us and you stand firm in Christ. He anointed us, and set his seal of ownership on us, and put his Spirit in our hearts as a deposit, guaranteeing what is to come."* 2 *Corinthians 1:21-22.*

When the Holy Spirit fills us and anoints us, He also seals us. In Biblical days, a signet ring or a cylinder that was engraved with the owner's name was worn. Anything that needed to be guarded or kept from being opened or that needed to be secured was sealed with this official mark.

The Spirit of God came to these men, and He comes to us, to seal a covenant between Him and ourselves. According to the terms of the covenant, we belong completely to God and He belongs completely to us. Almighty God places Himself at our disposal. He brings His own wisdom and power and might into our lives. He impresses His purposes on our hearts. He completes the good work He began in us as stated in *Philippians 1:6:* *"Being confident of this, that he who began a good work in you will carry it on to completion until the day of Christ Jesus."* The Lord Jesus Christ perfects us by filling us with His Spirit. This is the baptism that takes us from death into Life.

Then we are anointed for service to Him, and the Holy Spirit seals this covenant that has been made for eternity.

Now let us move on and consider the meaning of this experience in the lives of the disciples. Through this filling of the Holy Spirit, men on earth are literally joined to heaven through their union with Jesus. Paul wrote to the Corinthian Christians, *"He that is joined to the Lord is one spirit with him." 1 Corinthians 6:17.*

This is the central fact of the Christian faith. The person who is living one life with the God of glory is a Christian. This is the defining point. The person who joins a church, who studies the Bible, who admires the ethics of Christ, who agrees with Christian purposes, who catches the Christian vision, and holds to Christian principles is not an authentic Christian unless he/she is living one life with Jesus. This defies explanation, but it defines the truth we have been given.

"They were all filled with the Holy Spirit." The Spirit came from the Father, through the Son, and into them. At that moment, they began to live one life with Jesus. This is seen in *John 14:23.* Jesus replied, *"Anyone who loves me will obey my teaching. My Father will love him, and we will come to him and make our home with him."* This is what brought to them an entirely new vision of themselves. They saw themselves as God saw them. They saw a new vision of the world — God's vision of it. They gained a new vision of God, for their eyes were opened. Whereas they had been blind, now they could see. His outlook illuminated their minds. By the baptism of the Spirit of Christ, they had been given the mind of Christ. We find a comment on this truth in *1 Corinthians 2:1–16* Paul writes:

> *"When I came to you, I did not come with eloquence or human wisdom as I proclaimed to you the testimony about God. For I resolved to know nothing while I was with you except Jesus Christ and him*

crucified. I came to you in weakness with great fear and trembling. My message and my preaching were not with wise and persuasive words, but with a demonstration of the Spirit's power, so that your faith might not rest on human wisdom, but on God's power.

We do, however, speak a message of wisdom among the mature, but not the wisdom of this age or of the rulers of this age, who are coming to nothing. No, we declare God's wisdom, a mystery that has been hidden and that God destined for our glory before time began. None of the rulers of this age understood it, for if they had, they would not have crucified the Lord of glory. However, as it is written:

'No eye has seen, no ear has heard, no mind has conceived what God has prepared for those who love him. These are the things God has revealed to us by his Spirit. The Spirit searches all things, even the deep things of God. For who knows a person's thoughts except their own spirit within them? In the same way, no one knows the thoughts of God except the Spirit of God. What we have received is not the spirit of the world, but the Spirit who is from God, so that we may understand what God has freely given us. This is what we speak, not in words taught us by human wisdom but in words taught by the Spirit, explaining spiritual realities with Spirit-taught words. The person without the Spirit does not accept the things that come from the Spirit of God, but considers them foolishness and cannot

understand them because they are discerned
only through the Spirit. The person with the
Spirit makes judgments about all things, but
such a person is not subject to merely human
judgments, for: "Who has known the mind of
the Lord so as to instruct him?" But we have
the mind of Christ.'"

It was also true that through their hands Jesus was able to reach out and touch others. Through them He was able to travel to the ends of the earth. They were all joined to Jesus, and that meant that the localized body of Jesus of Nazareth was multiplied hundreds and thousands and ten thousand times ten thousand times over as the centuries have rolled by.

Every man, woman, boy, and girl that has entered into a relationship with Him through a new birth of the Spirit becomes a new body for Jesus! It is through us that He walks and talks and travels and reaches out to address the wounds and the weariness of humanity today. If this is true, then we need to look back once more over the pathway that Jesus walked. It is the pathway we are called to walk as we live one life with the Son of God.

The first step we observed was that of emptying Himself. What does that mean? It means that He laid aside His own rights. That is the story of the Spirit-filled life. We must lay down our rights. If we have taken the name of Jesus, if we proclaim Him as our Savior, if we have thereby received the Holy Spirit, yet we live a life that is centered on ourselves we blaspheme against the Holy Spirit. We must empty ourselves in order to be filled with Him. That is the simple truth.

Jesus showed us that lives that are filled by the Holy Spirit are lives of love that are lived out in word and in work. It is only as we share in His sacrificial love that we share in His work. The fullness of the Spirit gives us the ability to suffer with Christ on behalf of others. Paul wrote in his letter to the Galatians, *"My dear children, for whom I am again in the pains of childbirth until Christ is formed in you." Galatians 4:19.*

We all suffer greatly because others fall short of allowing Christ to live through them. Other people suffer greatly because we fall short as well. The kingdom of God comes as we allow His life to be poured out through us in joy and sorrow, in work and toil, and in pain and suffering.

Being filled with the Spirit carries with it the meaning and the reality of not only the suffering of the cross but also the power of the resurrection. It holds out to us the promise that we will reign with Jesus in the heavenlies. *Romans 5:17–21* clearly depicts this:

> *"For if, by the trespass of the one man, death reigned through that one man, how much more will those who receive God's abundant provision of grace and of the gift of righteousness reign in life through the one man, Jesus Christ!*
>
> *Consequently, just as one trespass resulted in condemnation for all people, so also one righteous act resulted in justification and life for all people. For just as through the disobedience of the one man the many were made sinners, so also through the obedience of the one man the many will be made righteous.*
>
> *The law was brought in so that the trespass might increase. But where sin increased, grace increased all the more, so that, just as sin reigned in death, so also grace might reign through righteousness to bring eternal life through Jesus Christ our Lord."*

We wait patiently with Him for ultimate victory; but in the meantime, we are given the strength and wisdom to live in victory over the circumstances that each day brings.

Finally, being filled with the Holy Spirit enables us to communicate His Spirit to others. If you would challenge that thought, turn with me to *John 7*. Here we find Jesus at the Feast in Jerusalem. Jesus said in John 7: 37-38, *"If anyone is thirsty, let him come to me and drink. Whoever believes in me, as the Scripture has said, streams of living water will flow from within him."* In *John 7:39* John adds, *"By this he meant the Spirit, whom those who believed in him were later to receive. Up to that time the Spirit had not been given, since Jesus had not yet been glorified."*

Christian service is filled with power only as the Spirit of God is communicated to other people. Only as we are filled with the power of the Holy Spirit can we be used by God to communicate this power to others. We receive the Holy Spirit so that, through us, it can be poured out to others.

What happened at Pentecost to the people who received the Holy Spirit? They began to show forth the wonder of God! They became people whose lives demonstrated His glory. Paul wrote to the Corinthians, *"Don't you know that you yourselves are God's temple and that God's Spirit lives in you? If anyone destroys God's temple, God will destroy him; for God's temple is sacred, and you are that temple."* 1 *Corinthians 3:16–17.* That is the meaning of Pentecost. Through Pentecost, their bodies were captured so that through them, in all their habits, in all their ways, in all their words and actions and reactions, and through all of their lives, God was seen through them.

The pouring forth of the Holy Spirit was not simply an event that occurred over 2,000 years ago on the day of Pentecost. It is the constant rushing forth of a river of life. It comes from the throne of God, and it flows out to the world through His saints who are themselves filled to overflowing with this gift of love and grace. What does that look like? Our family witnessed in my mother a life that exhibited just that.

Mother's life was exceptional by any measure! She was born in Oklahoma when it was still Indian Territory. When she was 6 years old her family moved to Fort Worth, Texas, where her father established a cattle business headquartered in the Fort Worth Stockyards. She graduated from Texas Christian University and taught in the Fort Worth Public Schools.

She married my father, and in doing so became a Presbyterian minister's wife. She was a stay-at-home mom until I started college. Then she went to work for General Mills where she was "Betty Crocker" for a time; the only person in the world who was authorized to sign that famous signature!

She returned to college and received a master's degree and then a doctorate in psychology, becoming the head counselor for the Fort Worth school system. For several years she authored a weekly column for the Fort Worth *Star-Telegram*. It was weekly comments on "The International Sunday School Lesson".

She was dearly loved and highly admired. However, in her mid 70s she discovered a way of living the Christian life that was new to her. It revolutionized a life that was already full and rewarding. She began to live a life of praise and thanksgiving IN ALL THINGS! As she began to actually live this out it caused her college age grandson to remark, "Whatever Grandmother has found, I want it!"

Mother lived independently into her mid 80s; then she came to live with James and me. She was with us almost two years. We agree that during that time we never heard one cross or complaining word. She brought kindness and appreciation and quiet joy and happiness into our home. Finally her need for 24-hour care led us to place her in an assisted living center. Small strokes robbed her of the ability to talk. For many months the only words she spoke were, "I love you."

The night mother died a new hospice nurse came to sit with us. I had been by her bedside for hours and she was sedated. After awhile the nurse said to me, "I have something I want to tell you, but I don't know how you will take it." She continued, "I belong to a church that believes in being able to discern spirits. What I want to tell you is that this woman is filled to overflowing with the Spirit of Love. When I placed my hands on her to take her vitals signs I became aware of it. Love is pouring from her." My response was, "I have no doubt that is true." That was her final testimony, a River of Love rushing forth in the midst of death.

It becomes clear that, just as with those disciples of old, we enter a realm of privilege when we are filled with the Spirit; but we also enter a realm of responsibility. We are living in the Pentecostal age, and we have no responsibility to ask for the Spirit of God. As surely as He lives, He lives in all who by faith have been born again to a living hope. But we do bear responsibility to obey the laws of the Spirit. The laws are of faith and of obedience. In proportion to our faith and our obedience the experience of Pentecost and its power within us and through us will increase.

To those who had not yet received the Holy Spirit, Jesus said, *"If you, being evil, know how to give good gifts, how much more shall your heavenly Father give the Holy Spirit to those who ask Him." Luke 11:11–13.* The gift of a new birth, the gift of a new life, the gift of the Holy Spirit of God: It is all ours for the asking, ours for the taking, ours for the believing, ours for the living!

Some of us received the Holy Spirit, but we have failed to follow the laws of the Spirit. The Holy Spirit works through our faith, and our faith has wavered. The Holy Spirit works through our obedience, and we are no longer obedient. The joys, the vision, the forces within us have become weak. The call to us today is to yield our lives to the Spirit. The Spirit is moving! The winds of God are blowing! The river of God is flowing! The fire of God is burning! In surrender, we will find once again the experience of Pentecost, the power of Pentecost, and the blessing of Pentecost poured out, not on us alone, but through us to our families and to the whole wide world.

One With You

Oh, to be One with You, Lord;
Oh, to be One with You.
Filled with the passion of Your love
In service to others true.
At peace in my spirit because of You,
With joy in my soul divine.
United with You for power to live
within Your will, not mine.

Think On These Things

Do you think you have been born by the Holy Spirit into a new consciousness? Explain your answer.

In what ways are you aware of an on-going experience of newness of life?

In what ways did the mission of the Lord Jesus Christ change with the coming of the Holy Spirit?

The first step Jesus took in God's plan for human redemption was to empty Himself. How did He do that?

The final step that was taken in God's plan for human redemption was to fill us. Explain what that means.

Why is it necessary to empty yourself, and how is that accomplished?

What happens when you are filled with the Holy Spirit?

What are the laws of the Spirit?   How can you learn to live in harmony with those laws?

How is your life experience impacted by the reality of these truths?

I think you will enjoy reading and thinking about *John 17*.

Lesson Six
What If I Do not Have The Holy Spirit?

TEXT: *"Did you receive the Holy Spirit when you believed?*

Acts 19:2, NIV

This is a very short text, and it contains a very great message. *"Did you receive the Holy Spirit when you believed?"* This verse contains two verbs, and the tense is the same in both of them. One poses a question (receive), and one is an affirmation (believe). Note: *"Did you receive?"*, and *"You believed."*

The importance of these verbs lies in the fact that some scholars have seen this verse as proof that the coming of the Holy Spirit is a second blessing. A very accurate translation would be, *"Coincidentally with believing, did you receive the Holy Spirit?"* The question was not whether these people had received a second blessing. Rather, it was a question concerning the nature of the first blessing. In order to understand the personal application, we must examine this verse in context, so let us read *Acts 18: 23–28.*

> *"After spending some time in Antioch, Paul set out from there and traveled from place to place throughout the region of Galatia and Phrygia, strengthening all the disciples.*
>
> *Meanwhile a Jew named Apollos, a native of Alexandria, came to Ephesus. He was a learned man, with a thorough knowledge of the Scriptures. He had been instructed in the way of the Lord, and he spoke with great fervor and taught about*

Jesus accurately, though he knew only the baptism of John. He began to speak boldly in the synagogue. When Priscilla and Aquila heard him, they invited him to their home and explained to him the way of God more adequately.

When Apollos wanted to go to Achaia, the brothers and sisters encouraged him and wrote to the disciples there to welcome him. When he arrived, he was a great help to those who by grace had believed. For he vigorously refuted his Jewish opponents in public debate, proving from the Scriptures that Jesus was the Messiah."

Here we have encountered Apollos. He was an Alexandrian by race, but he was a Jew, and he had been converted to Christianity. He was well-educated, and he had been instructed by word of mouth in the ways of the Lord. However, his knowledge and understanding were limited. All that Apollos knew was the baptism of John, and that was a baptism of repentance. He most likely had heard John preach, foretelling the coming of another whose shoelaces John was not worthy to untie. The one to come would baptize men with the Holy Spirit and with fire.

This was all that Apollos knew, but he taught this carefully. Now we read in our Scripture lesson that listening to him were Priscilla and Aquilla, a husband and wife who knew a lot more about the good news than Apollos did. They recognized the sincerity he brought to his teaching, but they also recognized what he lacked. They took Apollos aside and shared with him more fully and completely the message of Jesus. He accepted their instruction gratefully, and he traveled on to Achaia. It is obvious that his message had changed, and he taught persuasively that Jesus was the Christ.

In the early days of Apollos' preaching, he had taught what he himself had known and accepted: the baptism of John. John's baptism was a public renunciation of sin, a sign of repentance. Some who heard him received that baptism, but they knew of nothing more. The baptism of the Holy Spirit would be the sign of a new life. This is something for us to ponder, for no preacher or teacher can bring their hearers beyond the level of their own spiritual knowledge.

Apollos had been preaching in Ephesus, but he had moved on to Achaia, and Paul had arrived to preach in Ephesus. Paul immediately saw that something was missing! He could see that this church knew a great deal, but they had come just so far and there they had stopped. There are certain evidences of the Holy Spirit's presence in human lives that are easy to see, and Paul realized that those things were lacking. It may have been with a note of surprise in his voice that he asked, *"Did you receive the Holy Spirit when you believed?"* Their answer was, *"We have not even heard that there is a Holy Spirit." Acts 19:3.*

Today, over 2,000 years later, I wonder how many people in the churches of the world would give this very same answer! The Ephesians knew that John had preached that One was coming who would baptize them with the Spirit, but they didn't know whether or not that promise had been fulfilled. Paul asked them another question. He said, *"Into what were you baptized?"* They answered that it was into John's baptism. Paul then told them that they had not obeyed John's entire message. John told them to repent and accept a baptism of repentance, but he also told them that they were to believe on the One who was to come and who would baptize them with the Spirit of God.

Paul then told them of Jesus' coming, of His work and of His miracles, as well as of His death and resurrection and ascension. When they heard this they wanted to be baptized in the name of Jesus. Read *Acts 19:1-7:*

While Apollos was at Corinth, Paul took the road through the interior and arrived at Ephesus. There he found some disciples and asked them, "Did you receive the Holy Spirit when you believed?"

They answered, "No, we have not even heard that there is a Holy Spirit."

So Paul asked, "Then what baptism did you receive?"

"John's baptism," they replied.

Paul said, "John's baptism was a baptism of repentance. He told the people to believe in the one coming after him, that is, in Jesus." On hearing this, they were baptized in the name of the Lord Jesus. When Paul placed his hands on them, the Holy Spirit came on them, and they spoke in tongues and prophesied. There were about twelve men in all.

Their baptism was an act of faith. Paul laid his hands on them as a symbol of the coming of the Holy Spirit. As they were receiving baptism because they believed in Jesus, at that moment, the Holy Spirit fell on them.

Now watch, and listen, and see what happened. They prophesied. They spoke in tongues. From that day on, no one could ask them whether or not they had received the Holy Spirit when they believed. There were signs that He had come! The thing that was lacking was not lacking anymore. There was clear evidence of His presence. The inner life of the Spirit poured itself out in joy and praise and proclamation. They received the Holy Spirit. They believed on Jesus and on the entire message concerning Him. Up until that moment they had not received the Holy Spirit. They had believed on Jesus, but only within the narrow limits of John's message concerning Him. They had never heard the rest of the story.

As we examine our text in the light of this context, we can see what an important question this is for us today. Did we receive the Holy Spirit when we believed? Here in our Bible Study group I'm quite sure that all of us believe in Jesus. If I were to go around this table and ask each person here the same question, "Do you believe in Jesus?" I believe that each one of us in a natural, honest, truthful way would answer, "Yes." But this morning, I want us all to examine our hearts in the light of Paul's question. *"Did you receive the Holy Spirit when you believed?"* Do we have a belief that has resulted in the reception into our lives of the Holy Spirit of God?

Dr. Morgan wrote that he believed that if the apostles of the early church were to walk in and face many of the congregations that assemble every Sunday morning throughout the world, they would ask that question within the first 10 minutes. *"Did you receive the Holy Spirit when you believed?"* There are literally hundreds and thousands of people who, to some extent, believe in Jesus Christ who have never received the Spirit, who have never been baptized by the Holy Spirit, who have never been born-again by the Spirit of God.

These three terms all hold the same meaning. They refer to a new life lived in the power of a new Spirit who comes to live within us. Without the Holy Spirit we become people who are ruled by ethics, but we lack enthusiasm. We have principles, but no power. We desire more because we lack energy and conviction. This is a dangerous position to live in because it leads to what the writer of the letter to the Hebrews called becoming *"hardened"*. *Hebrews 3:13*. Bondage grows out of ethics that are casually accepted as true. Heartlessness grows out of principles that are obeyed without strong belief.

Cynicism grows out of a desire that is long unfulfilled for life on a higher plane.

We see this very thing happening everywhere. We believe on Jesus. We believe on Him with reverence. We don't take His name in vain. We have always attended church and Bible studies. We listen to the messages delivered by our pastors and our teachers. We may be the one delivering them! We are active in our church. We serve on committees. We sing the old hymns and the new choruses. We believe in the ideals of Jesus. We accepted them long ago, and we call ourselves Christians; but there is no fire in our hearts, no passion, no courage, no joy, and no songs.

This is what it means to be dead while we yet live. Intellectually we believe in Jesus, but we are spiritually dead. Our churches are crowded with such people. In truth, they have never been born again or baptized by the Holy Spirit. They have never received the Spirit of Christ, and if we were to ask them our question: "Did you receive the Holy Spirit when you first believed?", they would answer that they just aren't sure about the doctrine of the Holy Spirit. They might add that they don't really know whether or not the Holy Spirit is real, and besides that, if He is real, they believe He was only active in the early church.

For a moment, let's go back to our text. What was the fault of these people? They had come to a halt. John pointed them on to Jesus, but they had stopped short of embracing all of the truth concerning Him. They may not have been to blame. They may not have had the opportunity to hear the final facts about Jesus. The crucifixion may have wiped out the hope they had placed in Him. They may have only heard rumors of His resurrection and ascension. Be all that as it may, this we know for certain. After they had repented, they halted. They came to a standstill. They failed to take that second step that John had commanded of accepting the baptism of the Holy Spirit.

When Paul came and preached to them the full message of Jesus Christ, they believed in Him. They gave themselves to Him, and they felt the windows of their lives thrown open. They felt the joy and peace and power for which they had waited. It was all theirs when they abandoned themselves to Jesus!

What one thing is lacking in all who believe in Jesus, in all who have come so far as to recognize the glory and beauty of His purpose, to value His ideals and ethics? What one thing is needed? Just to take one more step, and that is, by an act of faith, to hand your life over to Him. Surrender yourself completely to Him.

These people expressed that act of faith in baptism. Dr. Morgan wrote that he did not believe that the method of expression was the important thing. No one believes that they received the Holy Spirit because they received water baptism, but through being baptized in the name of Jesus they expressed their faith in Him In answer to that faith, the Holy Spirit came upon them; and this is what He does for us.

This is what all of us need. In order to receive the Holy Spirit we must add faith to our repentance and confidence to our conviction, and these things must be held in relation to Jesus Christ. The living Christ has come. He asked the Father to send the Holy Spirit just as He said He would, and the Spirit has been poured out.

People make a mistake when they wait for years hoping that He will come. They wait in nights of lonely prayer. They wait while they attend conventions and retreats. They wait while they read books on the Holy Spirit. They grieve and they agonize. They beg and they plead, while all the time He is here! He has come to earth, and He wants to come into every one of our lives to lead us into all Truth and to bring Light and Glory.

What signs followed His coming? *"They spoke with tongues and prophesied." Acts 19:6.* That was their experience of Pentecost. The waiting and longing had led to the joy and gladness of receiving. Surely joy and gladness will be a great part of our individual experience of Pentecost. There is an enormous difference in believing in Jesus intellectually and in having belief that abounds in the love and joy and peace and courage that only the Spirit of God can give. The coming of the Holy Spirit brings to our lives the inner reality of the presence of God here and now, and we experience the gladness of receiving! What is that like for us?

Mother bought a plaque for me that hangs in my kitchen. Its inscription reads, "Joy is the most infallible sign of the presence of God." I have found that to be true! Hour by hour and day by day we can choose to live out of our spirits, thereby discovering a joy that is constant and authentic.

Along with the joy comes a lightness and strength of spirit. The well-known Chinese Christian, Watchman Nee, wrote of that. For a long time I didn't understand its meaning. Then an experience came my way that brought with it a heaviness of spirit. Along with that came overpowering weakness and the feeling that I could hardly put one foot in front of the other. A Bible verse came to my attention. Found in *Nehemiah 8:10* it reads, *"The joy of the Lord is your strength."* I discovered that as I kept my focus off of the distressing circumstances and on the presence of the Holy Spirit, I experienced deep joy that brought with it a buoyancy of spirit that greatly increased my strength!

In order to experience Pentecost, we must rest in God by living as if He is as good as his word. Back in the days when my grandfather worked in the Fort Worth Stockyards, business was all done on a handshake. There were no long and costly contracts drawn up. Business transactions worth hundreds of thousands of dollars were concluded only on a man's word. These men trusted one another!

Do we trust God? Do we take Him at His word? He has given us many promises, yet how seldom we accept them at face value. In *Matthew 7:7-8* we read, *"And without faith it is impossible to please God, because anyone who comes to him must believe that he exists and that he rewards those who earnestly seek him."* In *James 1:17* we read that *"Every good and perfect gift is from above, coming down from the Father of the heavenly lights, who does not change like shifting shadows. He chose to give us birth through the word of truth that we might be a kind of first fruits of all he created."* In *Hebrews 13:5* we read that God has said, *"Never will I leave you; never will I forsake you."* We have been given many such promises! The experience of Pentecost becomes ours when we choose to live as if they are true.

In our times of fellowship and prayer we can bring any request we have to God. We can tell Him what we would like to see done, but we also have the option of leaving the final choice to Him. I once received a card that said, "God always gives the best to those who leave the choice with Him." We can pray as Jesus prayed, *"My Father, if it is possible let this cup be taken from me. Yet not as I will, but as you will."* Matthew 26:39. The determination of my heart can be, "More than I want my own will, I want Yours. Choose what is best in the light of time and eternity, and with all my heart I will offer thanks."

I understand prayer to be a time to listen to the still small voice of the Holy Spirit, a time to gratefully take His promises to heart, and a time to offer praise and thanksgiving in all things. "Loving Heavenly Father; You are here this morning. How can I thank You enough for going before me today? You make a way where there is no way! Thank You for the amazing work of Your grace that is being carried out whether I can see it or not. I begin this day by bringing to You my praise and my love. In Jesus name, so be it!"

Joy was not the only sign of the Holy Spirit's coming. As we read further, we will discover that these early disciples created an atmosphere of proclamation. From that center, the word of God sounded forth throughout all of Asia. The idolatry that was entrenched in Ephesus was undermined, and before long we read of men burning their objects of witchcraft.

Today these same things are true. May we determine this hour to go a little further — a little further than confession, a little further than repentance, a little further than the long wait for something that never really comes, a little further into complete, absolute, joy-filled submission to Jesus Christ.

And then what? There will be praise and thanksgiving and prayer and proclamation. There will be an atmosphere in which the preacher can preach and the teachers can teach so that people will be saved. A center will form that will reach out first of all into our own families, and then into the neighborhood and the larger community and out into the whole world.

The Day of Pentecost did not come and go over 2,000 years ago. Today is the Day of Pentecost. The Spirit of God is here! If we are not praising and praying and proclaiming, it is because we are like the 12 men at Ephesus. We came just so far and no further. May all of us dare to go further! May we determine to go further! If, in answer to Paul's question, *"Did you receive the Holy Spirit when you believed?"* we must say, "No, I didn't," then receive Him right now.

How we can receive Him? The Holy Spirit is not received by seeking Him. We receive Him when we open our hearts to Jesus. In seeking Jesus, we receive the Holy Spirit. The Holy Spirit is the Spirit of God. The Holy Spirit is the Spirit of Jesus. We don't seek Jesus by subscribing to

113

Christian principles. We don't seek Jesus by listening to His teachings. We don't seek Jesus by believing Him to be our perfect example. We don't seek Jesus by trying to emulate Him.

We seek Him by surrendering to Him. We seek Him by putting our entire life at His disposal. We seek Jesus by trusting Him for yesterday and today and tomorrow and for all eternity. We seek Jesus by giving Him our entire life — by physically, mentally, spiritually and emotionally belonging to Him. We seek Him as we share His life!

This truth was brought home to me in an unusual way many years ago. Our three children were young, and my mother was sick and in the hospital. On Sunday morning James and I took the children and went to Sunday School and church. Then we came home to eat lunch. After our meal James said, "Honey, I'll clean up these dishes. You go on to the hospital and see how your mother is doing."

I got into the car and headed out, grateful for his offer. I was thinking about how much I loved and appreciated him, and I heard myself murmur aloud, "I am so thankful that he chose me to share his life." Immediately a response framed itself in my mind. It was the voice of God that I heard! I had no doubt about that, but it was not an audible voice. It was like a direct transmission from one mind to another. These were the words. "And I chose you to share My Life!" I was absolutely stunned and then awed. Tears of joy began to roll down my cheeks, and I cried all the rest of the way to the hospital. Oh, the wonder of it all. God Almighty chose me to share His life!

This is His word to every one of us. My Dad used to explain it this way. He said that he did not believe that God walks through the line of human history choosing some people and rejecting others. His understanding was that God chose to reveal His love and grace through mankind. We all have equal opportunity to share in His Life. In 2 *Peter 3:9* we read, *"The Lord is not slow in keeping his promise, as some understand slowness. He is patient with you, not wanting anyone to perish, but everyone to come to repentance."* He gave us free wills, and He will not overrule them. However, His offer stands good. Will we choose to share His Life?

If we have received the Holy Spirit we have one more responsibility and that is to yield to Him. Allow the fire, the power, the joy and the hope to rise up in you. Don't smother the song! Don't quench the Holy Spirit! Don't grieve the Holy Spirit! Don't resist the Holy Spirit!

If your answer to Paul's question is "Yes, yes, I have received the Holy Spirit. As surely as He lives, He lives in me", then be aware of the danger you are in. If you have received the Spirit, if the praise has come and the prayers have come and the words proclaiming the good news have come, then what is the danger?

The power and the reality of the Holy Spirit laid the foundation for the church at Ephesus. It was a great church, so wonderful that Paul wrote one of his last letters to it. But that was not the end of their story. The Lord in whom they had believed and through whom they had received the Holy Spirit wrote another letter to the church at Ephesus. He sent it through the apostle John from the island of Patmos. Through that letter, the tragedy unfolds. He writes, *"I have this against you, that you have left your first love." Revelation 2:4.*

Once again we hear the cry of God's heart over the lost love of people who had received the Holy Spirit. They had brought their praise to Him. They had offered their prayers to Him. They had proclaimed Christ. With the passing of time, rather than their love for Him growing, they had lost their first love. Other things had taken first place.

That brings us to another question. Have we lost our first love? Was there a time when our being was filled with the glory of God? Then life brought disappointment and sadness and confusion and loss, and somewhere along the way we quietly lost our first love. What did Christ say to that Ephesian church? He said, *"Repent and do the first works."* He was saying in effect, "Go back. Repent. Set the rudder of your will once again. Be transformed by the renewing of your mind. Get back to where you stood when you left me. Do once again the things you were doing when songs of praise rang out in your heart. Go back!"

There are multitudes today that see our churches as tombs of dead and lifeless people who feel nothing and know nothing of the very life of Christ pulsating through them. Such tragedy cannot be calculated! However, to those who belong to Him, every day offers great opportunities to honor Him with light and love and service. Every day can begin with a prayer of thanksgiving.

"Loving Heavenly Father, thank you for the gift of another day in which to come to know You better and love You more." May we thank our Heavenly Father for having sent the Holy Spirit to us, and may we live out our lives in the reality and the power and the blessing of His presence!

Cover Me
From Psalm 39

The heavens praise Your wonder.
You rule the raging seas.
Your hand is set over all the earth.
May Your hand ever cover me.

Cover me, oh cover me
With Your presence, Your love,
and Your grace.
Cover me, Lord, oh cover me
'Til the day I meet You face to face.

Think On These Things

Have you been taught about the Holy Spirit, or has this book been your introduction to this subject?

What happens to people who profess to be Christians, but who have never been born-again and received the Holy Spirit of God? On what do you base your answer?

How can you receive the Holy Spirit?

What does the Holy Spirit bring to your life?

What danger does this place you in?

How can your know if you have lost your first love?

How can you go back and reclaim it?

I think you will enjoy reading and thinking about *Ephesians 4:17-32.*

Lesson Seven
The Spirit of Life

TEXT: *"Through Christ Jesus the law of the Spirit of Life set me free from the law of sin and death."*

Romans 8: 2, NIV

In this lesson we are going to consider the Spirit of Life. What is the Spirit of Life? In the New Testament the Holy Spirit is described as *"the Spirit of Truth"*, as *"the Spirit of Promise"*, as *"the Spirit of Grace"*, and as *"the Spirit of Glory"*. However, the designation *"the Spirit of Life"* is all inclusive. It binds up all the other meanings into one. This phrase indicates the relationship God has to all of life.

Here we find two words. They appear together, and both of them refer to life. The word *"Spirit"* refers to life at its highest and best. Always where the reference is to God this word indicates Him to be the originating cause, the power that brought all life into being, the source and cause of existence, the origin of life in all of its forms.

The Greek word that is here translated *"life"* is interesting. It refers to the way in which life is revealed. It refers to the form that life takes. The Greek language is much more precise than the English. Whereas we have one word for *"life"*, the Greek language has at least two, and we are familiar with them because we have adapted them into our scientific usage. The words are *"bios"* and *"zoe"*. From them we have derived our words biology and zoology.

These two words represent two different ideas about life. They refer to two different perspectives on life. One fact about them that grabs our attention is that in

Greek classical literature they hold different meanings than they hold in the New Testament. That is unusual. Furthermore, the New Testament actually reverses their meanings. Why would that be? In what way is that significant?

In Greek literature the word *"zoe"* referred to the natural side of life. It would be almost accurate to say it referred to the animal side of life. The word *"bios"*, however, held within it a spiritual component, a set of moral principles, and a meaning of ethical value. This contrast between the two words is maintained throughout all Greek literature.

However, when we come to the New Testament we find that the order is consistently reversed. When Jesus refers to life, when the New Testament writers refer to life, the higher word in Greek thinking and writing is assigned the lower usage, and the lower word is given the higher usage. Therefore, *"zoe"* holds spiritual meaning, and *"bios"* holds animal meaning.

Why would this be? What importance does it hold? What message is it meant to convey? We know that this was a change that occurred quietly, but powerfully. When Christian writings are put together and compared we find this usage to be consistent. It is clear that Jesus adopted the change, and then the New Testament writers conformed to it.

This is important because behind this change of word lies a change of thought. It expressed a new thought about life; a new and different concept as to the way life began. The Greeks saw life in a particular way. While the New Testament writers understood their perspective, at the same time they saw the source and cause of existence quite differently.

Christians came to recognize the sacredness and holiness that lies behind every form of life. They came to see that behind all of life lies a Divine purpose and plan and design. They understood that the intention is holy. Every realm of life always and everywhere is due to the work and the activity of the Holy Spirit.

During those early days of Christianity it was perfectly understood that man had fallen into willful rebellion. In the book of Romans Paul wrote what is the most terrible revelation in all of literature of what sin has done to the heart of man. Here we read Romans 1:18-32:

"The wrath of God is being revealed from heaven against all the godlessness and wickedness of men who suppress the truth by their wickedness, since what may be known about God is plain to them, because God has made it plain to them. For since the creation of the world God's invisible qualities — His eternal power and divine nature-have been clearly seen, being understood from what has been made, so that men are without excuse.

For although they knew God, they neither glorified Him as God nor gave thanks to Him, but their thinking became futile and their foolish hearts were darkened. Although they claimed to be wise, they became fools and exchanged the glory of the immortal God for images made to look like mortal man and birds and animals and reptiles.

Therefore God gave them over in the sinful desires of their hearts to sexual impurity for the degrading of their bodies with one another. They exchanged the truth of God for a lie, and worshiped and served created things rather than the Creator — who is forever praised. Amen.

Because of this, God gave them over to shameful lusts.   Even their women exchanged natural relations for unnatural ones. In the same way the men also abandoned natural relations with women and were inflamed with lust for one another. Men committed indecent acts with other men, and received in themselves the due penalty for their perversion.

Furthermore, since they did not think it worthwhile to retain the knowledge of God, he gave them over to a depraved mind, to do what ought not to be done. They have become filled with every kind of wickedness, evil, greed, and depravity. They are full of envy, murder, strife, deceit and malice. They are gossips, slanderers, God-haters, insolent, arrogant and boastful; they invent ways of doing evil; they disobey their parents; they are senseless, faithless, heartless, and ruthless. Although they know God's righteous decree that those who do such things deserve death, they not only continue to do these very things but also approve of those who practice them."

The picture presented here is of a people who glory in what should be their shame!

This was not what Life was meant to be! In contrast to all of this, in a powerful and pervasive way Christianity took hold of a word that in Greek literature always held within it the taint of sin and changed its meaning because Christian thought was changed by the coming of Jesus. Because of Him, Christians began to see life as holy. Furthermore, they recognized Jesus as the embodiment of the Spirit of Life!

What does that have to do with us? All to often Christian people forget the relationship of the Spirit of God to all of life! The Bible never loses sight of the fact that all life is the result of the direct action of the Spirit of God.

The Spirit of God is the Spirit of Life. We first find that meaning in Genesis *1:1-2*. *"In the beginning God created the heavens and the earth. Darkness was on the face of the deep, and the Spirit of God moved on the waters."* The Bible gives us a spiritual explanation to all of original creation.

The ancient Hebrew heard God in the thunder. He saw God in the lightening. To him, the fragrance of the flowers was the result of the inbreathing of God's Spirit. Its delicate beauty was the workmanship of God. He saw God behind all life, and with the coming of Jesus that perspective was confirmed.

To those who live and walk in the Spirit of Christ all creation is seen to be of God. Dr. Morgan wrote that he would not suggest that we find God through nature. He wrote that mankind can't begin with nature and climb from there up to God. However, we can begin with God and enter into the secrets of nature with a deep appreciation of the way in which its beauty and majesty reflects its creator. It reminds us of the fact that the same Spirit that brings transformation in the natural world is bringing constant transformation to our characters and to our lives. Nature calls us to remember the God who is present.

I have experienced that in an exceptional way this summer. Several years ago a special man came into our life. He keeps our yard for us. We told Michael that we are no longer able to travel, and that our yard is our place of recreation and refreshment. We wanted him to expand it into a beautiful garden. He is quite an artist, and he continues to develop our two acres into a lovely area.

As winter melted into spring, and spring into summer the changing panorama of blooms often brought me to tears! I began to see and experience our garden in a new way. I wrote about it in my journal.

"A garden is a place of mystery. It is a place set apart. It calls me from a life of noise and frantic activity to a place and time of tranquility. It provides a bridge between the familiar world of an ordinary life and the contemplation of timelessness and eternity.

A garden is filled with the Spirit of Life! It is made up of things seen and things unseen. Therein lies its mystery. Hidden life stirs, and expands, and eventually bursts forth from its prison. It grows! It develops from bud to flower to fruit to death, only to be resurrected anew in its season. Many forms of life remain hidden under leaves and in the grass, insects of every kind! Deep in the soil microscopic forms of life break down the soil and enrich it.

The garden stands as a microcosm of my own life. My life also consists of what is seen and what is unseen. Both are part of the reality of being. The visible world always originates in the invisible world. The garden is a demonstration of this principle. It conveys God's design and His purposes. It speaks to me with the voice of God, but in order for me to hear Him I must honor Him with quietness and solitude."

Seeing God in all is a wide outlook, but going forward in our meditation we will narrow it down and focus our attention on how a limited perspective affects us. So often our focus rests on us as we are rather than on us as we were meant to be. We get lost in our shortcomings. We lose sight of the Divine ideal. We lose the vision of what we were born for. We no longer know what God created us to be.

The Bible gives us two views of the Divine ideal as it was expressed in human life. We find there the picture of the *"first Adam"* and the *"last Adam"*. In *"the first Adam"* we are able to see what the Spirit of God brings into human life. In *Genesis 2:7* we read that *"Jehovah breathed into his nostrils the breath of life, and man became a living being."* Here we find our nature revealed. We are both dust and Deity. We are made of dust and then in-breathed by God. As the source of all life, He is The One who bequeaths life. We are of the earth, yet as offspring of the Spirit of God we are also of the heavens. This is a great mystery. It defies all explanation. It is beyond our ability to understand.

We are told that the first thing that Adam was conscious of was the awareness that he was subject to God. Secondly, he was conscious of the environment around him. He was able to name the animals. He was able to till the soil. He could will to cooperate with God.

In *Genesis 2:8–9* we read, *"Now the Lord had planted a garden in the east, in Eden; and there he put the man he had formed. And the Lord God made all kinds of trees grow out of the ground – trees that were pleasing to the eye and good for food. In the middle of the garden were the tree of life and the tree of the knowledge of good and evil."*

Genesis 2: 15 -16: "The Lord God took the man and put him in the Garden of Eden to work it and take care of it. And the Lord God commanded the man, 'You are free to eat from any tree in the garden; but you must not eat from the tree of the knowledge of good and evil, for when you eat of it you will surely die.'"

Genesis 2:19-20: "Now the Lord God had formed out of the ground all the beasts of the field and all the birds of the air. He brought them to the man to see what he would name them; and whatever the man called each living creature, that was its name. So the man gave names to all the livestock, the birds of the air and all the beasts of the field."

This story is one of beauty and glory! The Spirit of God bestows life in all of its forms, and He enlists mankind to join with Him in the joy and privilege of protecting and tending and naming it. However, before long the beauty of the story was marred. Adam and Eve chose to disobey God by eating of the tree of the knowledge of good and evil. Sin entered the picture, and by sin came death. Century after century would pass before we would come into the presence of *"the last Adam"*. Jesus Christ is the last Adam.

As we have already seen, the story of the human life of Jesus is the story of the truth that the Spirit of God is the Spirit of Life. Every bit of the natural human life of Jesus was Life in the Spirit. It was by the power of the Spirit that He existed as a human being. The last Adam came into life once again by the dust of the earth and by the in breathing of God. He grew by means of the Spirit Life. He grew physically and mentally and spiritually by means of the Spirit of God.

In His ministry He was anointed by the Spirit. *"When all the people were being baptized, Jesus was baptized too. And as He was praying, heaven was opened and the Holy Spirit descended on Him in bodily form like a dove. And a voice came from heaven: 'You are my Son, whom I love; with You I am well pleased.'"* Luke 3: 21-22.

He was driven into the wilderness by the Spirit to be tempted. *"Jesus, full of the Holy Spirit, returned from the Jordan and was led by the Spirit in the desert, where for forty days He was tempted by the devil."* Luke 4:1.

He returned to His ministry in the power of the Spirit. *"Jesus returned to Galilee in the power of the Spirit, and news about Him spread through the whole countryside. He taught in their synagogues, and everyone praised Him."* Luke 4:14-15.

His miracles were wrought by the same Spirit. *"The Spirit of the Lord is on me, because He has anointed me to preach good news to the poor. He has sent me to proclaim freedom for the prisoners and recovery of sight for the blind, to release the oppressed, to proclaim the year of the Lord's favor."* Luke 4: 18-19.

He passed through the mystery of His death, and on the morning of His resurrection He took up His life again by the power of the Spirit. He returned to human consciousness and stayed for 40 days with His disciples.

"Then the eleven disciples went to Galilee, to the mountain where Jesus had told them to go. When they saw Him they worshiped Him, but some doubted. Then Jesus came to them and said, 'All authority in heaven and on earth has been given to me. Therefore go and make disciples of all nations, baptizing them in the name of the Father and of the Son and of the Holy Spirit, and teaching them to obey everything I have commanded you. And surely I am with you always, to the very end of the age.'" Matthew 28:18-20.

Luke tells us that Jesus instructed them about the Holy Spirit long before the Spirit was poured out on them. *"Jesus said to them, 'This is what I told you while I was still with you; everything must be fulfilled that is written about me in the Law of Moses, the Prophets and the Psalms.'*

Then He opened their minds so they could understand the Scriptures. He told them, 'This is what is written: The Christ will suffer and rise from the dead on the third day, and repentance and forgiveness of sins will be preached in His name to all nations, beginning at Jerusalem. You are witnesses of these things. I am going to send you what my Father has promised; but stay in the city until you have been clothed with power from on high.'" Luke 24:44-49.

We see that from the very beginning the life of Jesus was life in the Spirit. It was not spiritual life as something distinct from human life. It was LIFE! It was essential life! It was basic life! It was spiritual life in the broad and simple and profound sense that all life is life by the Spirit of God. Turning to John we read that *"In Him (Jesus) was life, and the life was the light of men."* John 1:4.

This conception of what life is reveals what a terrible thing sin and death is. If we had a life that existed apart from the Spirit of God it would still be grossly ungrateful to deliberately sin. But the life we live is lived in the power of the Spirit of God. It is by His grace that we live and move and have our being. Can you imagine how terrible it is to take this incredible gift of life and use it in ways that hinder God's kingdom; in ways that block His will; in ways that insult His love and hinder His purpose?

We speak of being filled with the Spirit, of being anointed by the Spirit, of being regenerated through the Spirit and of living a spiritual life. These expressions do not refer to rare experiences, and they do not call us to live in some realm for which we were not made. These are words that call us back to what is normal and natural. They define the fulfillment of our creation. When we are born again by the Spirit of God we do not become something other than ourselves. Through our second birth, through being born again, we become ourselves. We come to ourselves. We find ourselves. We discover our destiny.

The terms Jesus lays out are hard, but necessary. Before He can baptize a person with the Spirit of Life, that person must consent to die. By that I mean we must give up our right to ourselves. And then what? We find the life that we lost. Jesus explained it when He said, *"He that finds his own life shall lose it; and he that loses his life for my sake shall find it." Matthew 10:39.* The life that is found is not some other life. It is not a life that is strange or foreign. It is my own life in which Jesus Christ has been crowned Lord of all!

The filling of the Holy Spirit, the anointing of the Holy Spirit, the baptism of the Holy Spirit breaks the power of sin. Rebellious areas of our lives are reclaimed for God. It is not just that the desert parts of our lives are handed over to God. It is that in being possessed by Him all areas break out into life. They bud out and blossom and bear fruit. Every area of our lives will find full and complete and beautiful expression by, in, and through Him!

Through the lineage of Adam we are born with spirits that are dead. Death is not extinction; it is separation. Our spirits are separated from God and cut off from relationship and fellowship with Him. It is through

129

the second birth which is a spiritual rebirth that we find the true meaning of our first birth. Through our second birth the Holy Spirit brings us back into fellowship with Himself. He brings our lives back into harmony with God. He brings us to an understanding of our own lives, and into the realization of all that He created us for. It is the Spirit of Life that renews us and restores us to our Creator's first intention.

All people owe their first life to the Holy Spirit, to the Spirit of life. All too often we fail to recognize and acknowledge that. Then we lose His energy, we lose His enlightenment, we lose the light that He brings. If we return to Him, He will return to us. He will remake us as Scripture expresses it, as new creatures. *"Therefore, if anyone is in Christ he is a new creation; the old has gone, the new has come!"* *2 Corinthians 5:17.*

The Spirit of Life takes possession of us as we place our faith in Jesus. He fulfills God's meaning and purpose for us. May we yield ourselves completely to Him so that His plans for us will be completed. May we be people who are filled with Life and Light and are baptized with power. May we be people who live to God's honor and glory. May we be people whose lives demonstrate for all to see just how clear and open, how generous, how abundant, how courageous, how magnificent, and how vast in range and scope life really is! May the whole burden and the hope of our work and of our lives rest on the matchless gift of the Holy Spirit of Life!

Creation

The sky of blue, the clouds above
Express our great Creator's love.
Oh God, I pray my life may be
An expression of your love for me.

The stars that blaze above my head,
The sun that shines in blazing red
Show forth Your might and majesty,
Yet You come to make Your home in me.

Lord, lift me up that I may be
A token to Your royalty.
Lord, take my life and let it be
Lived all for You, Lord;
All for Thee.

Think On These Things

What is the meaning and the significance of the Holy Spirit being the Spirit of Life? How does this fact hold the secret to the growth and transformation God has promised for your life?

Who are you? What are you? What is the nature of the mystery that is your life? What do you base your answer on?

How is the story of the human life of Jesus an unveiling of the truth that the Spirit of God is the Spirit of Life? How does this give you the pattern for your metamorphosis?

Before you can receive the Spirit of Life you must be content to let go of the spirit of death. In other words, you must be willing to lose your own life for Christ's sake. How can you do that? Why would you want to do that? What would hold you back from taking that step?

In losing your own life, what do you find? Are you living today in the power and revelation of that truth?

I think you will enjoy reading and thinking about *2 Corinthians 3.*

Lesson Eight
The Witness of The Holy Spirit

TEXT: *"I tell you the truth; it is for your good that I am going away. Unless I go away, the Counselor will not come to you; but if I go, I will send him to you. When he comes, he will convict the world of guilt in regard to sin and righteousness and judgment; in regard to sin, because men do not believe in me; in regard to righteousness, because I am going to the Father where you can see me no longer; and in regard to judgment, because the prince of this world now stands condemned."*

John 16:7-11 NIV

At some point in the life of all human beings there comes a time of spiritual awakening. A spiritual awakening can be defined as an awareness of things of the spirit, a realization that we are all primarily spiritual beings. It is a deep inner stirring of what makes us uniquely who we are. It is the consciousness of God, and it brings with it an awareness of righteousness. With that awareness comes awareness of sin, and of impending judgment.

This can occur again and again in our lives without producing any permanent result. A new awareness of the spiritual side of life does not necessarily produce renewal or regeneration of the spirit, or the beginning of a new life. A spiritual awakening occurs when we are confronted by the fact of a spiritual side to life. Suddenly we know it exists and we know it is real!

Spiritual awakenings occur under many different circumstances. Sometimes they happen in the most ordinary way on the most ordinary of days. Sometimes they happen when we are walking our dog, or working in our garden, or taking out the trash! Sometimes they happen when we are singing hymns, or hearing a Bible message, or reading our Bibles. Sometimes they happen during times of stillness and silence and meditation. Sometimes they happen in times of great danger. The most hardened people cry out to God if their boat is sinking or their plane is going down.

The immediate result of the awakening is very predictable, and we have already referred to it. It is three-fold. We think of God, and of His righteousness. We think of ourselves, and of our sin; and then we think of judgment. If these thoughts are faced honestly, they result in a double consciousness. We have two thoughts at almost the same time. The thought of sin brings with it a thought of the paralysis of being unable to overcome it. The thought of righteousness brings with it a sense of the impossibility of ever attaining it. The thought of judgment brings with it the thought of the guilty verdict that we pass on our own lives, and of the sentence that we feel is hanging over our heads.

These thoughts are not peculiar to Christianity. Mankind has always known the fact of sin, the fact of righteousness, and the fact of judgment. These things were known long before Jesus came, but when He came He said that the Holy Spirit would come to "convict the world of sin, and of righteousness and of judgment". What unique testimony does the Holy Spirit bring to us of these things?

With His coming He put these three facts of life into a brand new perspective. He saw each one of these facts in relationship to Jesus Christ. Listen again to the words. *"The Spirit will convict the world ... of sin, because they believe not on me; of righteousness, because I go to the Father, and you behold me no more; of judgment, because the prince of this world has been judged."*

Here Jesus revealed the fact that with His coming sin suddenly held a new center and a new responsibility.

"Of sin, because they believe not on Me." Here we find the new center. Instead of dealing with us on the basis of all our individual sins, the thousands of ways in which sin presents itself in and through our lives, the Holy Spirit would deal with the root of all sin, the center from which it all comes. That center is our unbelief. It is our unwillingness to accept the sacrifice Jesus made to offer us a new life.

Furthermore, He reveals how He will deal with sin; not in the places where Jesus is not known, but in the hearts and lives of those who have heard of Him and been offered the opportunity of believing in Him. Jesus' word is that once the Holy Spirit has brought His unique ministry into our lives, sin becomes a different thing.

In what way is that true? We most often think of sin as rebellion against the laws of God, the plans of God, the purposes of God. People speak of their sins and of the sins of others. They may name passion and lust, lying and cheating, stealing, gossiping, backbiting, laziness. We all know the list can go on and on, but most people would say that the root of all sin is rebellion against the government of God. There is some truth in that, and in line with that thinking we need to add that sin is not an illness to be excused. It is not an inheritance to be pitied. It is not an unfortunate bad habit. It is turning our backs on God and focusing instead on ourselves. It is refusing to accept Jesus as the only way to God. Read what Jesus said in *John 14:1-6:*

"Do not let your hearts be troubled. Trust in God, trust also in me. In my Father's house are many rooms; if it were not so, I would have told you so. I am going there to prepare a place for you. And if I go and prepare a place for you, I will come back and take you to be with me that you also may be where I am. You know the way to the place where I am gong."

*Thomas said to him, "Lord, we don't
know where you are going so how can we
know the way?"*

*Jesus answered, " I am the way and
the truth and the life. No one comes to the
Father except through me."*

I dare say there is not one person sitting here today
who can say, "I believe on Him. Always, in all ways and
at all times, I believe Him. I believe every promise in the
Bible. I trust every path He is marking out for me.   I
believe on Him fully and completely!"

We often think we believe. We fervently declare
our belief, but do we believe?   Let me tell you of a
wonderful young woman who sometimes came to see me.
She was about to finish college. For several years she had
been dating a Christian, and often we had prayed together
over their relationship. I had been deeply touched by the
way she voiced her commitment to God's plan for her life.
Her prayers were always that God would choose His best
for her.

One night I received a call from her. Between sobs
she told me that the young man had broken off their
engagement.   She was devastated.   As I listened I
wondered where her faith had gone. Did she suddenly
believe that God had not heard her prayers? Did she think
He was not answering? Did she think He had gotten busy
with someone else and had forgotten her? What was she
thinking?

Another young couple, in love with one another,
and in love with the Lord have wanted a family for a long
time. The past 5 years have been marked by the financial
expense and the emotional roller coaster of the myriad of
treatments that exist today for infertility. As time has
passed their once bright testimony has been almost
silenced. They have gradually withdrawn from friends.
They voice disappointment, frustration, discouragement,

and doubt. Is God listening? Does He care? Where is He? Will He ever give them children? What good is prayer?

We are all familiar with these stories, aren't we? They have been our stories. I would guess that at some point in every life they have been our stories!

Where is the point in your life at which you no longer are believing on Him? What is it you can no longer trust Him for? The promises He makes to us are incredible. The promises He has already fulfilled on our behalf are stunning! His promises for our futures are astounding! Hear the words of scripture.

"Know that the Lord has set apart the godly for Himself. The Lord will hear when I call to Him." Psalm 4:3.

"For the Lord God is a sun and shield; the Lord bestows favor and honor; no good thing does He withhold from those whose walk is blameless. O Lord Almighty, blessed is the man who trusts in You." Psalm 84:11-12.

"My children will not toil in vain or bear children doomed to misfortune; for they will be a people blessed by the Lord, they and their descendants with them. Before they call I will answer; while they are still speaking I will hear." Isaiah 65:23-24.

Keep your lives free from the love of money and be content with what you have, because God has said, "Never will I leave you; never will I forsake you." So we say with confidence, "The Lord is my helper; I will not be afraid. What can man do to me?" Hebrews 13:5.

"Don't be deceived, my dear brothers, every good and perfect gift is from above, coming down from the Father of the

heavenly lights, who does not change like shifting shadows." James 1:16-17.

What is our response? The Holy Spirit speaks it. *"Of sin, because they believe not on me."* Of sin, because My Word means nothing to them. Jesus lived a life that was directly opposed to doubt. His dedication in all things was to the throne of God. He did not question what His Father said or willed.

We know the truth of that, and we accept it. We know that Jesus' life was lived amid imperfection, yet it was perfect. We know it was lived surrounded by impurity, yet it was pure. We know that amid treason, He was loyal. We know that His surrender and dedication to His Father never wavered. And we know that through His death He made our sin His own. In taking responsibility for our sin He provides for us far more than forgiveness. He gives us far more than a pardon. He provides justification. He has done away with all of the guilt of our past, and He is waiting to energize all of the weakness of the present. He will strengthen our hearts to believe!

How often we ignore that offer. We fall back into old habit patterns of doubt and fear; and when we do, that is sin. It is the sin of unbelief, and there is no other sin left, because He has dealt with them all. The sins of the past are all gone. In the eyes of God it is as if they have never happened. I remember Mother teaching one Sunday morning that one thing God cannot do is remember our sin. *"As far as the east is from the west, so far has he removed our transgressions from us."* Psalm 103:12.

There is no sin that exists in our present life that He cannot deal with. I remember a woman who came to my parents for counseling. For years she had been a faithful and active member of our church. She had never married. She was a quiet and unassuming woman, but now guilt was destroying her life. For a long time she had harbored a secret; an ongoing affair with a married man. Finally she could live with it no longer. She broke off the relationship, and confessed it as sin to God and to her pastor. However, she felt certain that God could never forgive the immorality involved or the lie she had lived.

Daddy pointed her to many of God's promises on forgiveness, but she couldn't accept them. She couldn't believe them. Finally he said to her, "Do you honestly believe that any human being can commit a sin that can exhaust the grace of almighty God?" That statement flooded her heart with understanding, and she was able to gratefully accept God's full forgiveness.

Think of it! Complete redemption is at our disposal, but when we fail to accept it by believing it we remain slaves to our sin. Our unbelief leaves us guilty of all the sins that have accrued against us. The one central sin that keeps me bound by all the others is the sin of failing to believe God. *"Of sin, because they believe not on me."* If we went around the table this morning I imagine each of us could tell of some particular sin that we struggle with, but the Holy Spirit would tell us today that is not our sin! The sin is that we do not believe Him. If we did we would abandon our lives to Him. The power of sin would be broken. The guilt would be gone. We would be living lives of confidence and victory.

The sin lies in refusing the remedy He provides. The sin lies in doubting His word. The sin lies in rejecting His promises. The sin lies in living in fear. The sin lies in giving up hope. The sin lies in our mourning over sin that we cannot cure. That is an insult to God and it brings grief to the Holy Spirit, for Jesus paid the price for the remedy. I once heard a simple example will suffice. What if a friend lay dying and you heard of a sure cure for her illness. You rushed out to purchase it, and then hurried to her house to deliver it. However, she refused the remedy. She never appropriated what you provided, and eventually she died. Did she die of the disease? In one sense she did, but the remedy was sure, and she died because she refused the remedy.

God's redemption is total or it is nothing. God does not pick and choose the sins that He will forgive. His remedy for sin is sure and certain. He forgives all of our sins. If we turn our backs on God's redemption we are guilty of all the sins arrayed against us. The moment we choose to believe God, sin must loosen its hold on us.

This brings us to the new responsibility that was placed on mankind when Jesus came, and that is to believe on Him. In *John 6:28-29* we find the account of Jesus' disciples asking Him how they can do the works of God. *Then they asked Him, "What must we do to do the works God requires?" Jesus answered, "The work of God is this: to believe in the one he has sent."*

Following that we find the testimony of the Holy Spirit to righteousness. He "will convict the world in respect ... to righteousness, because I go to the Father." We will see that Jesus is revealed here in two ways. First, He is the perfect pattern. Secondly, He is all sufficient power.

Let us note that here we find presented a new ideal of righteousness. We discover that righteousness does not consist of simply keeping commandments. It is not just obedience to the laws of God. Rather we see that righteousness grows out of the relationship we have with God. It grows out of a heavenly relationship that causes earthly relationships to be holy and sacred. We see that righteousness will issue out of a life that is rooted and grounded in the Heart of God, and the Love of God.

In *Ephesians 3:14-21* we find this powerful prayer written by Paul:

> *"For this reason I kneel before the Father, from whom his whole family in heaven and on earth derives its name. I pray that out of his glorious riches he may strengthen you with power through his Spirit*

in your inner being, so that Christ may dwell in your hearts through faith. And I pray that you, being rooted and established in love, may have power, together with all the saints, to grasp how wide and long and high and deep is the love of Christ, and to know this love that surpasses knowledge — that you may be filled to the measure of all the fullness of God. Now to him who is able to do immeasurably more than all we ask or imagine, according to his power that is a work within us, to him be glory in the church and in Christ Jesus throughout all generations, for ever and ever! Amen."

This is a righteousness that is resolved in surrender. Jesus is speaking in *John 5:30* and *John 6:38*. Hear His words.

"By myself I can do nothing: I judge only as I hear, and my judgment is just; for I seek not to please myself but Him who sent me." John 5:30.

"For I have come down from heaven not to do my will but to do the will of Him who sent me." John 6:38.

Look at these principles at work in the life of Jesus. Jesus said, *"He (the Holy Spirit) will convict the world in respect to righteousness, because I go to the Father."* What is He saying?

He is saying that His relationship is with His Father. He is saying that His life on this earth was centered on His Father; on His love, His tenderness, His compassion, His ways, His plan. He is saying that His life here flowed out of His Father's will. He is saying that He came from His Father, and He is going home to His Father. He is saying that His home is with His Father. He is saying that His Father's home is His home. The new ideal of righteousness He is presenting is the truth that righteousness does not come out of morality, or out of our own personal sense of right or wrong. Righteousness flows from a relationship with the Father.

The message here is that the Holy Spirit Himself delivers us from false conceptions of righteousness. He shows us its true meaning, and the message is that it is righteousness that causes us to feel completely at home with God. Righteousness loves what He loves, and hates what He hates. Righteous people are fully at ease with God. Righteous people are completely at home with God.

The Holy Spirit reveals to us the enormous chasm that exists between our own morality and the righteousness of Jesus Christ. If we measure our morality by a court of law we may appear quite respectable. However, standing before Almighty God and measuring against His righteousness there exists the distance between heaven and hell.

Jesus said, *"I go to the Father."* These are simple words of human speech. They were spoken when He was living here. He was walking dusty roads. He was seeing the same things we see; flowers blooming and trees budding, clouds in the sky, changes in the seasons. He lived here, but at the same time, He was living there. He was forever at home with His Father. He lived His life here within the bosom of His Father. That is righteousness! Jesus said, *"Of righteousness, because I go to the Father."* This is the pattern. We live here, but at the same time we are always to be with our Father!

But that is not the end of the story. If this revelation of Jesus' righteousness were all that we had we would be without hope. There are people who say that Jesus is their ideal, but in seeing the glory of His righteousness we all see how far short we fall.

But Jesus meant more than that. When Jesus said *"I go to the Father,"* He meant, "I go to the Father for you."

"I tell you the truth; It is for your good that I am going away. Unless I go away, the Counselor will not come to you; but if I go, I will send Him to you." John 16:7.

God's standard of holiness was met by the purity of His life. He returned to heaven as the perfect man, but He returned, wounded, with scars in His hands, on His feet, and in His side; mute evidence of the cost of our redemption. The song of heaven shouts out His victory as He is welcomed home, but His scars tell the old, old story and forever will proclaim how He makes it possible for the lost to be found and the impure made holy and the prodigal to return home. *"Now the Spirit has come to convict the world in respect ... of righteousness, because I go to the Father."*

The Spirit convicts us of a new pattern of righteousness, and declares a new power through which we can become righteous and holy. If we miss this we miss the heart of the good news. What constitutes our salvation? By what right will we someday stand in the light of God's grace? Certainly we will be there because God pardons our sin. Secondly, and just as important it will be because by His power He makes us perfectly righteous.

It is not as if we are already made perfect, but the One who began a good work in us will complete it. It is not God's plan to lead back to His dwelling place an army of crippled, deficient, incompetent spiritual beings. So, what is He going to do? To a weary world this is what the Father says concerning righteousness. *"The true pattern is seen in My Son. The true power lies in the Holy Spirit; and you shall be changed!"*

These scriptures speak that truth:
"Being confident of this, that he who began a good work in you will carry it on to completion until the day of Christ Jesus." Philippians 1:6

"Not that I have already obtained all this, or have already been made perfect, but I press on to take hold of that for which Christ Jesus took hold of me. Brothers, I do not consider myself yet to have taken hold of it. But one thing I do; forgetting what is behind and straining toward what is ahead, I press on toward the goal to win the prize for which God has called me heavenward in Christ Jesus." Philippians 3:12-14.

"We proclaim Him, admonishing and teaching everyone with all wisdom so that we may present everyone perfect in Christ. To this end I labor, struggling with all His energy, which so powerfully works in me." Colossians 1:28-29.

"But you have come to Mount Zion, to the heavenly Jerusalem, the city of the living God. You have come to thousands upon thousands of angels in joyful assembly, to the church of the firstborn, whose names are written in heaven. You have come to God, the judge of all men, to the spirits of righteous men made perfect, to Jesus, the mediator of a new covenant, and to the sprinkled blood that speaks a better word than the blood of Abel." Hebrews 12:22-23.

"May the God of peace, who through the blood of the eternal covenant brought back from the dead our Lord Jesus, that great Shepherd of the sheep, equip you with everything good for the doing of His will, and may He work in us what is pleasing to Him, through Jesus Christ, to whom be glory for ever and ever. Amen." Hebrews 13:20-21.

Now we are coming to the end of our text, and what does the Spirit say about judgment? *"Of judgment, because the prince of this world has been judged."* Here we have looked at a new and different emphasis on sin. We have looked at a new and different emphasis on righteousness.

Here we also find a new and different emphasis on judgment. In the gospel of the resurrection we find hope and comfort, but surely it holds the severest condemnation that has ever been pronounced against sin. On that Easter morning long ago God singled out Jesus as the only approach to Himself. In the sight of all mankind God was saying, *"This is the Man I accept. This is My Anointed One. This is the way."* But He was saying more.

As Dr. Morgan points out, God was also saying that all men who are unlike Jesus He rejects. The message is that it is only as we are like Him that we can be accepted by God. It is only as we are like Him that we can hope to rise as He arose and ascend to heaven as He ascended. God's plan for us is that we be made like His Son!

The following verses confirm that truth:

"For those God foreknew He also predestined to be conformed to the likeness of His Son, that He might be the firstborn among many brothers." Romans 8:29.

"The first man Adam became a living being; the last Adam, a life-giving Spirit. The spiritual did not come first, but the natural, and after that the spiritual. The first man was of the dust of the earth, the second man is the man from heaven, so also are those who are of heaven. And just as we have borne the likeness of the earthly man, so shall we bear the likeness of the man from heaven." 1 Corinthians 15:45-49.

The cross of Christ and the resurrection of Jesus stands as God's verdict against sin. *"The prince of this world has been judged."* On the morning of the resurrection the verdict was disclosed and the sentence was passed. This One is accepted. All unlike Him are rejected; and judgment is pronounced against the prince of this world.

Note who is judged: the prince of this world. The master of worldliness. And what is worldliness? It is all that never reaches out for God. The world and its prince has been judged and pronounced a failure and condemned to its own death. Because he has been judged already, his captives have been set free; but they must choose freedom.

The Spirit does not come to convince us that judgment is coming. He comes to tell us that judgment has come. If, in spite of that we choose to live in a world bounded by our own truths rather than by God's Truth, if we choose the testimony of our own emotions and intellect rather than the witness of God's word, if we make this world and our present circumstances the focus of our lives, then we will share the hell of the prince of this world, both now and in the world to come.

The testimony of the Holy Spirit that we have studied today is the most serious and searching declaration we will ever find concerning sin and righteousness and judgment, yet at the same time it is the most hopeful. By the witness of the Holy Spirit I learn that not only are my sins all paid for and forgiven, but the sins that bound me need bind me no more. God does not call me to run from a strong foe who is trying to overtake me, and who will dog my footsteps for as long as I live. The Spirit's word to me is that Satan's power has been broken, and I have been delivered.

The question hangs in the air. Do you believe that? Do you really believe? If you do, your life will be lived in aggressive expectation of all God's promises being fulfilled! Our lives are telling the story.

What we believe is being confirmed every day by how we are choosing to live. May the Holy Spirit help us to see the truth of our lives, and to respond wholeheartedly to

God's matchless grace by believing that God always keeps His word. By His mercy and grace may we be able to say, "Lord, I believe!"

Fill Us With Your Life
Give Us Your Love

God, our Father, Our shelter from storm;
Mighty stronghold, a steadfast arm.
God of hope, of grace, of love.
God of creation Who rules above.

Jesus, Anointed One, the Ancient of Days;
Redeemer and High Priest,
Worthy of all praise.
Lamb of God, Savior and King.
Bright morning star, to You we sing!

Spirit of truth, the Word in us abides!
Comforter, the One who guides.
Voice of the Almighty;
Pure, gentle Dove;
Fill us with Your Life,
Give us Your Love!

Think On These Things

How does this lesson describe a spiritual awakening? Have you ever had such experience? What do you remember about it? Over time, did it produce any change in your life? Explain your answer.

How is it true that spiritual awakenings are not unique to Christianity? What three facts of life are part of the experience?

In what ways did the coming of the Holy Spirit put these facts into an entirely new perspective? In what way does sin now hold a new center and a new responsibility? What is the new center? What is the new responsibility?

When and how did your new life in Christ begin?

Think of a sin that you struggle with. Can you explain how the center of this sin is unbelief?

Are there areas in your life in which you no longer trust God's involvement, His answers, and His plan? Can you explain what brought you to that place? Are you willing to accept the new responsibility that God places on you? In what way will that bring you to a new beginning?

If worldliness is all that never reaches out for God, in what rooms of your heart or in what corners of your life are you worldly?

How did the Holy Spirit bring a new ideal of righteousness? What does it consist of?

What new and different emphasis did we find on judgment? Who has God judged? How does that judgment affect every one of us?

I think you will enjoy reading and thinking about *I John 2:1-17.*

Lesson Nine
The Fruit of The Holy Spirit

TEXT: *"The fruit of the Spirit is love, joy, peace, patience, kindness, goodness, faithfulness, gentleness, and self-control. Against such things there is no law."*

Galatians 5:22, NIV

I believe it was A. W, Tozer who said that the most important factor in determining a person's life is the picture they hold of God. That was an astounding statement to me! I had never thought of that. Some people see God as One to be feared; as a Being that wrecks vengeance on our lives. They live in constant fear of Him. In some societies and in some cultures this fear led people to sacrifice their own children in hope of escaping God's retribution.

This was brought home to us in a powerful way when we went on a family vacation and visited Chichen Itza on the Yucatan Peninsula of Mexico. This site is one of the great centers that contains Mayan ruins.

In the course of a tour we were taken down a dirt path to view a cenote. This is a deep sinkhole that is known as the Sacred Cenote, or the Well of Sacrifice. The Mayans believed that it was an entrance to the underworld. It was the site of offerings and human sacrifices that were made to appease Chaac, the Mayan rain God. During the 1960s, National Geographic led an expedition to dredge it. The yield was over 30,000 artifacts, and the bones of around 200 people, mostly children.

Even today there are societies in which bizarre things are practiced to try to gain favor with God or to escape judgment. Recently we have witnessed suicide bombers, who hope thereby to go straight to heaven. In the history of mankind there has existed only one religion in which God sacrificed Himself on behalf of human beings. That is the Christian religion.

However, it is true that in our own society there are many who see God as One to be feared. They live in daily dread of what God is going to do to them. Anything they perceive as "bad" they blame on God. Why does God allow bad things to happen to good people? Why did He allow the terrorist attack of 9/11? Why did He allow our economy to implode? Why did God do this to us?

On the other hand there are those who see God as totally irrelevant. They take no account of Him. They live as if God does not exist. Others live lifetimes of surrender to a God they love and trust. We could pursue this line of thought further, but you see the picture. The concept we hold of God determines how we live our lives!

Perhaps the most sublime statement the Bible makes concerning God is the simple statement expressed by the Apostle John in just three little words; *"God is Love."* It is a statement that inspires awe concerning what Christianity offers mankind; a God who is Love! Paul goes on to tell us in *Galatians 5* that not only is God Love. The fruit of His Spirit is love. This one brief sentence gathers up the entire truth of the Christian message. When this is written, everything is written. *"The fruit of the Spirit is love."* This is our text today, and it is taken from *Galatians 5:22*.

In *Galatians 5* the Apostle Paul describes the difference that exists between the works of our flesh and the fruit of the Spirit. Let's turn to *Galatians 5:16-26*. Here I will quote from the translation *The Message:*

"My counsel is this: Live freely,
animated and motivated by God's Spirit.

Then you won't feed the compulsions of selfishness. For there is a root of sinful self-interest in us that is at odds with a free spirit, just as the free spirit is incompatible with selfishness. These two ways of life are antithetical, so that you cannot live at times one way and at times another way according to how you feel on any given day. Why don't you choose to be led by the Spirit and so escape the erratic compulsions of a law-dominated existence?

It is obvious what kind of life develops out of trying to get your own way all the time: repetitive, loveless, cheap sex; a stinking accumulation of mental and emotional garbage; frenzied and joyless grabs for happiness; trinket gods; magic-show religion; paranoid loneliness; cutthroat competition; all-consuming yet never-satisfied wants; a brutal temper; an impotence to love or be loved; divided homes and divided lives; small-minded and lopsided pursuits; the vicious habit of depersonalizing everyone into a rival; uncontrolled and uncontrollable addictions; ugly parodies of community. I could go on. This isn't the first time I have warned you, you know. If you use your freedom this way, you will not inherit God's kingdom.

But what happens when we live God's way? He brings gifts into our lives, much the same way that fruit appears in an orchard: things like affection for others, exuberance about life, serenity. We develop willingness to stick with things, a sense of compassion in the heart, and a conviction that a basic holiness permeates things and

155

people. We find ourselves involved in loyal commitments, not needing to force our way in life, able to marshal and direct our energies wisely.

Legalism is helpless in bringing this about; it only gets in the way. Among those who belong to Christ, everything connected with getting our own way and mindlessly responding to what everyone else calls necessities are killed off for good, crucified.

Since this is the kind of life we have chosen, the life of the Spirit, let us make sure that we do not just hold it as an idea in our heads or a sentiment in our hearts, but work out its implications in every detail of our lives. That means we will not compare ourselves with each other as if one of us were better and another worse. We have far more interesting things to do with our lives. Each of us is an original."

(You may want to read this in a more familiar translation.)

We are going to examine the statement found in *Galatians 5:22: "The fruit of the Spirit is love."* We will look at it from three perspectives, moving quickly over the first two, and spending most of our time on the last.

The first thing we see is that this declaration reveals the method of Christianity when it uses the word fruit. *"The fruit of the Spirit is love."* The word *"fruit"* presupposes life. Apart from life there can be no fruit. It takes life to produce fruit. The word *"fruit"* also presupposes cultivation. Fruit comes to perfection through cultivation. Finally, fruit is food. Fruit supports and sustains life. In these simple thoughts concerning fruit we have a revelation of the whole systematic method of Christianity; the principles, the rules, and the laws that govern it.

The Apostle Paul writes of *"the fruit of the Spirit"*, and he writes of *"the works of the flesh"*. Dr. Morgan wrote that fruit and works can be compared by saying that fruit speaks of the garden while works speak of the factory. What does that mean? I think we encounter some interesting thoughts here.

Our works exist within the realm of death. Everything that human beings do is doomed to decay and disintegration. Everything is doomed to destruction. Mankind's finest works exist within the realm of death. We can take as an example this house we are meeting in this morning. In order to build it, men had to handle dead materials. A tree that once stood in the forest with rising sap and budding life was of no use to the builder. That tree had to die before the builder could begin his work. Furthermore, before the builder put his finishing touches to this house, mother nature was beginning to tear it down. The process of decay had already set in. It is a simple fact that even as we work our work is being destroyed.

This is the picture Paul gives us concerning the works of the flesh. Paul tells us that the best work anyone can do apart from Christ is a thing of decay. It will break apart. It will pass away. It will perish. It cannot abide. It is a thing of death.

But fruit, ah, it is different! It is a thing of life! We know that by observation. It holds within itself the properties of perpetual life. All fruit contains within itself the potential for unceasing reproduction; *"the tree bearing fruit, wherein is the seed thereof, after its kind." Genesis 1:11-12.* Fruit is a thing of life, and Christianity is a thing of life. Its final fruit is love, and it cannot be made. It cannot be manufactured. It cannot be willed. It must grow.

Fruit has to be cultivated. If you allow fruit trees to run wild the fine qualities of the fruit are lost. Fruit trees must be pruned and watered and fertilized and sprayed for insects and protected against cold weather. Fruit trees must be tended to.

The fruit of Christianity is love. Love will grow to maturity only as it is cultivated, only as it is tended to, and only as it is provided with the elements necessary for its growth. Now, who is going to cultivate it? Are we responsible for cultivating our own fruit? Who is going to care for it? Thankfully, that is not left up to us, but to our Heavenly Father. Jesus said, *"I am the true vine and you are the branches and my Father is the husbandman." John 15:1.*

Cultivation has as its goal the bringing about of the perfection of the fruit. In our own lives, that perfection is to be found in our becoming like Christ. That is the good work that God begins in us. That is the maturity He would bring us to.

Ephesians 4:11-16 speaks of this:

"It was He who gave some to be apostles, and some to be prophets, some to be evangelists, and some to be pastors and teachers, to prepare God's people for works of service, so that the body of Christ may be built up until we all reach unity in the faith and in the knowledge of the Son of God and become mature, attaining to the whole measure of the fullness of Christ. Then we will no longer be infants, tossed back and forth by the waves, and blown here and there by every wind of teaching and by the cunning and craftiness of men in their deceitful scheming. Instead, speaking the truth in love, we will in all things grow up into Him who is the Head, that is, Christ. From him the whole body, joined and held together by every supporting ligament, grows and builds itself up in love as each part does its work."

158

James and I have good friends who had a peach orchard in Waco, Texas. For many years it was their pride and joy! When the peaches reached their peak of perfection Brad and Virginia would call us and say, "Come on down!" Off we would go to pick peaches. And what peaches they were; big and juicy and flavorful. They were a delight!

Sometimes people would comment to Brad that he must be making a lot of money on his peaches. He would laugh at that, and tell them that it cost him everything he could get his hands on to produce such peaches. The cost of such perfection ran high!

The day came when Brad and Virginia sold their peach orchard and moved away from Waco. They were saddened when the new owner failed to maintain it, and before long it fell into ruin. The new owner told the whole story when he said that producing fine fruit was too hard, and the cost was too high, and it took too long. All of that was true; but you see, Brad had cultivated his peaches out of love.

It is out of love that the Holy Spirit patiently cultivates the fruit of our lives. It is a good work that He began, and He will complete it! *"I am confident of this, that He who began a good work in you will carry it on to completion until the day of Christ Jesus." Philippians 1:6.*

We have already said that fruit is nourishment. Fruit is food. It is sustenance, but Dr. Morgan points out that the sustenance suggested here is not for us. It is for God. *"God is Love,"* and what God hungers for is our love. Listen to the Old Testament prophets. From beginning to end we hear the sighing, the wailing of God after the love of His people. Dr. Morgan wrote of how he thought of the Old Testament prophets as men of wrath and thunder who were renouncing sin and proclaiming judgment and holiness. When he gave himself over to an extended study of their writings, his life was deeply changed forever.

What he discovered behind all of that was the infinite longing of God for the love of His people. He discovered how deep was God's disappointment that people did not love Him! We hear His cry in *Genesis 3:9* as the Father calls, *"Adam. Adam, where are you?"* We hear it in *Hosea 6:4* and *Hosea 11:8*. *"How shall I give you up, Ephraim? How can I hand you over, Israel?"* We find the cry of God's heart over and over again throughout Scripture, and we understand that cry, don't we?

Is there a one of us around this table this morning who has not felt that to be the cry of our heart toward someone we love? *"How shall I give you up? How shall I give you up?"* As we read it in Scripture this is not the voice of an arresting policeman. It is the cry of a Father who has lost His child. It is the lament, the sob of pain, the wail of a Being who is hungry for the love of His children.

We believe God is here this morning. The Husbandman is here, in His own garden. What is it He is looking for? He is looking for the fruit of the Spirit. There is only one fruit of the Spirit, and that is love. He sees our hearts, and that is the fruit He longs to see flourishing there. He wants to find the fruit of the Spirit which is for the sustenance of God's own heart in its hunger for our love. For many years my first thought before my eyes have opened in the morning has been, "Father, I love You. I love you! Thank You for granting me another day in which to learn how to love You more."

We have looked at the method of Christianity, which is growth toward maturity. Passing on to another thought, we find revealed in our text the force, the energy, the dynamic of Christianity in the word *"Spirit"*. What is Christianity? It is Life itself. How is that Life generated? Through being born of the Spirit. How is that Life cultivated? Through the ministry of the Spirit.

Christianity produces the fruit that nourishes God's own heart! What an astounding thought; and how does that fruit finally come to full maturity? Love comes to its complete fruition as my spirit is filled with the Spirit of Christ. *"If any man has not the Spirit of Christ, he is none of his."* *Romans 8:9.* If we have the Spirit of Christ, we have the Spirit of Love; and, wonder of wonders, God finds the answer to the hunger of His heart ... in me!! The fruit is produced by the Life that the Holy Spirit gives to us, and the fruit is love. The life that is in us will produce the fruit that will be revealed through us.

Always when I teach this I am taken back to that fall when James brought some plants home to put in our garden down at the creek. His construction company had been paving a street in a residential neighborhood, and he had gotten to know a lady who had a beautiful yard. He commented to her that I loved flowers. On his last day of work she presented him with some plants that she said would produce pretty purple flowers.

We put them into the ground with high expectations, and as spring arrived I examined the garden every day to see if any green shoots were pushing through the dirt. The day came when, with great excitement I took James to see that our flowers were coming up! He took one look at them and said, "Honey, that is not our flowers. That is poison ivy!" The life that was in those plants was the life that came out of those plants. What was in them was revealed through them, and sure enough, the life in the plants coming up was poison ivy! We sprayed that poison ivy, and several weeks later our flowers came up. Some 25 years later they still fill that flower bed with vibrant color every summer.

We are now coming to the plain meaning of our text. *"The fruit of the Spirit is love,"* but that is not all that this verse says. As we continue to read we find a problem. The verse reads, *"The fruit of the Spirit IS"* and then there are eight words that follow the word *"love"*. They are joy, peace, long-suffering, kindness, goodness, faithfulness, meekness, and temperance.

Recognizing what seems to be a grammatical error the verse has at times been quoted, *"The fruits of the Spirit ARE."* That is grammatical, and it has led to a common supposition that there are nine fruits of the Spirit, but that is not what the text is really saying. How can we get to that?

We have already said that the full and final fact concerning the Christian experience is expressed in these seven words: *"The fruit of the Spirit is love."* Love is not a small word. It cannot be easily passed over. It is not a sentimental word, and we see here that Paul writes down the word *"love"*, and then there surges over him a realization of the component parts of that word. It is as if that one word brings into play a magnificent orchestra. As Paul listens he can pick out the different notes of the music: joy, peace, patience, kindness, goodness, faithfulness, meekness, and self control.

These are the harmonies of the Christian life. I believe we can prove that if we truly have love we have all of these attributes, and if we don't have love we lack them all. Love is an all-inclusive word. The words that follow explain its meaning. Let us look at these words and see if we can discover the beauty of this music; then let's see if we find every one of these notes to be a reality in our own hearts and lives.

First of all, joy. It is not descriptive of an ecstasy that overtakes us now and then. It doesn't indicate a special red-letter day. Such experiences are to be valued, but joy has little to do with infrequent experiences. It is a simple word that describes a cheerful attitude, gladness, common delight. It speaks of a wonderful quality of life that brings with it light and peace and happiness. It is a consciousness that sings through the most ordinary day. Only a life that is filled with love finds a song of joy in the midst of the ups and downs of life. Joy is the consciousness of love.

Peace. The word that is translated here from the Greek indicates harmony that follows a battle. It is opposing forces that have been brought into accord. It is freedom from conflict. It is an end to hostilities. It is serenity. It is quiet assurance. What power is equal to that assignment? None other than love! We said that joy is the consciousness of love. Peace is the confidence of love.

Patience. In some translations you will find this word translated "long suffering." It is the quality of endurance. In *1 Corinthians 13*, Paul wrote that, *"Love suffers long and is kind."* We know what it means for a person to be short tempered. Patience is the opposite of that. Patience means being long tempered. Probably the most long-tempered people in the world are mothers, because they love so much. *"Love bears all things, believes all things, hopes all things, endures all things."* *1 Corinthians 13:7*. That is the story of a mother's love. That is long temperedness. Patience is the habit of love.

Kindness. The Greek word used here refers to service; and it means *"usefulness in small things."* Once again it is an attitude of life, and it helps us to see the small things that will comfort, encourage and help. It is the willingness to do simple things to help others. It is love that helps us to see these things and go meet the need. Kindness is the activity of love.

Goodness is just goodness! It is a word we don't use much anymore, but it is a great word. It's a word that we use in the nursery. We tell little children to be good. What makes them good? In the long run it is not the severity of punishment. That may hold a child in line for a while, but ultimately it is love that inspires all goodness.

When I was a child it was Daddy who exercised what he called discipline and I called punishment. Most often that raised indignation in me, and outright rebellion.

However, Mother could simply say, "Honey, that would disappoint me." Those words were all I needed to hear, for I loved her, and I never wanted to disappoint her. Jesus said, *"If you love me you will keep my commandments."* That is the total philosophy of goodness. That is the inspiration of goodness. I cannot grieve the one I love.

How can we define goodness? We say it is a great word because holiness and righteousness are both bound up in it. What is holiness? It is rightness of character. What is righteousness? It is rightness of conduct. Goodness encompasses both of these attributes, and goodness is the nature of love.

Our next word is faithfulness. To be faithful is to keep faith. It is loyalty and reliability. It means being true to your word. It means keeping your promise. It means being dependable. What binds us to our word? Nothing but love. It is finally love that holds us to our duty. It is love that makes infidelity impossible. Love will stand watch over all our actions. Faithfulness is the measure of love.

We come now to the words gentleness or meekness. They refer to genuine humility. We can accurately describe it as unconscious humility. The gentle, the meek, the humble person does not know that she is humble. She is able to keep doing what is commonplace and what is drudgery with an unconsciousness of self.

In one of my mother's lessons she wrote, *"Jesus greatest miracle was not, as is often supposed, the raising of Lazarus from the dead. Rather, it was the veiling of deity with flesh, and the continued humbling of Himself to ordinary creature existence."* The best known Scripture reference on this is *Philippians 2: 5-8. "Your attitude should be the same as that of Christ Jesus: Who, being in very nature God did not consider equality with God something to be grasped, but made Himself nothing, taking the very nature of a servant, being made in human likeness.*

And being found in appearance as a man, he humbled Himself and became obedient to death, even death on a cross! Therefore God exalted him to the highest place, and gave him the name that is above every name, that at the name of Jesus every knee should bow, in heaven and on earth and under the earth, and every tongue confess that Jesus Christ is Lord, to the glory of God the Father." Gentleness, meekness, humility is the quality of love. It is the character of love.

Now for our final word: self control. It is love that inspires us to self control. If someone were to come to one of us and tell us that we should not do this or indulge in that we might well be inclined to say or to think, "You need to mind your own business and leave me alone." But if someone comes to us and says, "You have another generation coming after you, and they are watching how you walk. They want to see how you do." Suddenly, out of love, our attitude is changed. We discover that the prayer of our heart is expressed in that beautiful song, "May All Who Come Behind Us Find Us Faithful."

Self control grows out of the Holy Spirit's interpretation of love as it is impressed on our hearts and is carried over into our lives. Self control is love's victory.

So here we have it; a portrait of Jesus! If we have love we have all of these things. Joy is love's consciousness. Peace is love's confidence. Patience is love's habit. Kindness is love's activity. Goodness is love's quality. Faithfulness is love's measure. Gentleness is love's character. Self-control is love's victory. As we live it out we will see that each quality works with and increases the power of all the other qualities, bringing to the Christian life perfect unity and integration. The only way to ever know and experience this love is through handing our whole being over to the Holy Spirit. He is The One who communicates the Life of Jesus to us. He wants to fill us with Himself!

This is an astounding truth, and as we hear it we

may find ourselves thinking, "How can this be?" Jesus said, *"If you will do, then you will know."* John 7:17. Remember God's order. *"First the stalk, then the head, then the full corn kernel in the head."* Mark 4:28. The fruit of the Spirit will be perfected only through time and cultivation.

Our Father is the Husbandman, and the process of bringing the fruit to maturity is hard, and the price is high, and it takes a long time; but He does it out of Love. Ultimately, the love that is produced in us and through us is given back to Him and out to others, bringing joy and satisfaction to His heart.

When I was just a bride my mother said to me, "Honey, we all learn to love in the way we have been loved. If you will love James the way you want him to love you, some day he will be able to return that kind of love to you." That is what God has done for us. He has loved us the way He wants us to love Him, and it is His will that we grow in the ability to return that love to Him and to share it with others in His name. *"We love Him because He first loved us."* I John 4:19.

As we come to a close, let me summarize it in this way. The Husbandman works to perfect his crop and bring it to harvest. He clears the land. He kills out the weeds. He breaks the soil and plows the ground. He sows seed. He fertilizes. He irrigates. He sprays for insects. He does everything he can to maximize the potential for growth. He provides the elements necessary for growth, and He also provides the growth. All of this God does on our behalf.

If that is God's part, what is our part? We must be able to appropriate the elements that are necessary for spiritual growth. How can we do that? We could easily devote an entire lesson to that question, but several verses lay out the foundation for it all. We find them in *Ephesians 3:16-21:*

"I pray that out of His glorious riches He may strengthen you with power through His Spirit in your inner being, so that Christ may dwell in your hearts through faith. And I pray that you, being rooted and established in love, may have power, together with all the saints, to grasp how wide and long and high and deep is the love of Christ, and to know this love that surpasses knowledge -- that you may be filled to the measure of all the fullness of God. Now to Him who is able to do immeasurably more than all we ask or imagine, according to His power that is at work within us, to Him be glory in the church and in Christ Jesus throughout all generations, for ever and ever! Amen."

What do we discover here? Our part is to stay rooted and grounded in God's Love! Right now it is August in Texas, and we are experiencing temperatures of more than 100 degrees almost every day. Last spring I planted some beautiful container gardens. A few days ago I noticed that although we had watered and tended them faithfully they were beginning to droop. Within a day or two some of them had died!

Upon close inspection I discovered that although I had planted them deep into the soil, the roots had worked their way to the surface where they now lay exposed. There was nothing to anchor the plants. They had fallen over. Furthermore, they could no longer take in water or nourishment. They were not rooted and grounded. They were not properly related to the soil, so they had died.

The fruit of the Spirit will only grow out of the soil of God's Love. Our part is to remain rightly related to Him; rooted and grounded in His Love. What does that mean? How can we do that?

The secret lies in the relationship we maintain with God through prayer and through His Word. God gives Himself to us through His Word. We give ourselves to God through our prayers. Both prayer and the Word revolve around God. As we make Him the one object of our desire we share blessed fellowship with Him. Rooted and grounded in Him there is an interchange of thought and Love and Life, and we grow! We can't help growing! We can't keep from growing! In this way the fruit of the Spirit becomes our present possession, fulfilling our destiny and bringing honor and glory to God!

God We Adore You

God above the heavens we adore You.
Spirit of our God, we bring your praise.
Jesus, Son of God, we pledge our honor and our love.
To God the Three-In-One our voices raise.

We bring You glory. We bring You glory.
You call us by Your name.
We bring You honor. We bring all glory
To our God, Who will forever reign!

God above the heavens we adore You.
Spirit of our God, we bring you praise.
Jesus, Son of God we pledge our honor and our love.
To God the Three-In-One our voices raise!

Think On These Things

Can you share an example of how your concept of God determines how you live your life? Can you share your concept of God?

Discuss the meaning of those three little words; God is Love. Explain how it is that they touch our lives in such a profound way.

Can you explain how the entire truth of Christianity is bound up in the message that the fruit of the Spirit is Love? How does this truth impact your life?

How does Paul describe the difference between the works of the flesh and the fruit of the Spirit?

Have you ever thought of the fruit of the Spirit as it is produced through your life as being sustenance for God? The fruit is love; love for God, love for ourselves, and love for each other. What significance does that hold for you? How can you live that out?

What is the energy and dynamic that lies behind spiritual growth?

Explain how we come to a mature love.

How would you explain the harmonies of the Christian life as we find them defined in our text?

Explain the part of the Holy Spirit in producing the fruit of the Spirit in our lives.

Explain our part.

I think you will enjoy reading and thinking about 1 Peter 2.

Lesson Ten
The Burning Heart

TEXT: *"Did not our heart burn within us, while he talked to us along the way, while he opened to us the Scriptures?"*

Luke 24:32, KJV

It may well be that the greatest need we have today is for hearts that burn within us with love and passion for Christ. That is a great need in the life of us as individuals, and it is a great need in the life of the Christian church. All too often we try to hold to our principles, but we lack true enthusiasm. We sometimes see attempts that are not genuine to manufacture or stir up emotion. That makes a lot of noise, but it lacks power.

As we hold these opening remarks in mind we will read the story of two men who quite unexpectedly encountered the living Christ! It took place after the resurrection of Jesus, and today we are living in post-resurrection times, so the story we find here will hold a great application for our lives.

In *Luke 24:1–12* we read:

"On the first day of the week, very early in the morning, the women took the spices they had prepared and went to the tomb. They found the stone rolled away from the tomb, but when they entered, they did not find the body of the Lord Jesus.

While they were wondering about this, suddenly two men in clothes that gleamed like lightning stood beside them. In their fright the women bowed down with their faces to the ground, but the men said to them, "Why do you look for the living among the dead?

He is not here; He has risen! Remember how He told you, while He was still with you in Galilee: 'The Son of Man must be delivered into the hands of sinful men, be crucified and on the third day be raised again.' Then they remembered His words.

When they came back from the tomb, they told all these things to the eleven and to all the others. It was Mary Magdalene, Joanna, Mary the mother of James, and the others with them who told this to the apostles. But they did not believe the women, because their words seemed to them like nonsense. Peter, however, got up and ran to the tomb. Bending over, he saw the strips of linen lying by themselves, and he went away, wondering to himself what had happened."

Now, the scene changes. Let us try to imagine ourselves right now walking along that dusty road that ran from Jerusalem to Emmaus. Read here *Luke 24:13-32:*

"Now that same day two of them were going to a village called Emmaus, about seven miles from Jerusalem. They were talking with each other about everything that had happened. As they talked and discussed these things with each other, Jesus himself came up and walked along with them; but they were kept from recognizing him.

He asked them, "What are you discussing together as you walk along?" They stood still, their faces downcast. One of them, named Cleopas, asked him, "Are you only a visitor to Jerusalem and do not know the things that have happened there in these days?"

"What things?" he asked.

"About Jesus of Nazareth," they replied. "He was a prophet, powerful in word and deed before God and all the people. The chief priests and our rulers handed him over to be sentenced to death, and they crucified Him; but we had hoped that he was the one who was going to redeem Israel. And what is more it is the third day since all this took place.

In addition, some of our women amazed us. They went to the tomb early this morning, but didn't find his body. They came and told us that they had seen a vision of angels, who said he was alive. Then some of our companions went to the tomb and found it just as the women had said, but him they did not see."

He said to them, "How foolish you are and how slow of heart to believe all that the prophet has spoken! Did not the Christ have to suffer these things and then enter his glory? And beginning with Moses and all the Prophets, he explained to them what was said in all the Scriptures concerning himself.

As they approached the village to which they were going, Jesus acted as if he were going farther. But they urged him strongly, "Stay with us, for it is nearly evening; the day is almost over." So he went in to stay with them.

When he was at the table with them, he took bread, gave thanks, broke it and began *to give it to them. Then their eyes were opened and they recognized him, and he disappeared from their sight. They asked each other, "Were not our hearts burning within us while he talked with us on the road and opened the Scriptures to us?"*

The Christ who appeared to these men was the same person He was before His crucifixion, but at the same time He was forever changed. We are followers of this same Christ, and this story has great value for us because just as many today have lost their passion, these men had lost their passion. They had not altogether lost their love. They had not altogether lost their faith, but they had lost their fire!

First let's accept an introduction to them, and then consider what their story reveals to us that they possessed. One of the men was named Cleopas, and the other was a nameless disciple. They knew what had happened to Jesus in Jerusalem. They knew that He had suffered a disgraceful death. That had brought bitter disappointment to them, but these two men still loved their Lord. Their faith in Him had not failed. We are talking here about that quality of faith which saves a man. They were thinking about Him and talking about Him as they were walking down the road that day.

Suddenly Jesus Himself joined them, but they did not recognize Him. They thought He was simply another stranger who happened to be traveling that same way. To them this appeared to be nothing more than a chance encounter.

Jesus fell in with them, and began talking with them. He asked them what they were talking about that caused them to look so sad. Listen to their answer. *"Are you the only person in all of Jerusalem who does not know what has happened there these past few days?"* And Jesus said, in order to draw them out, *"What things?"* Now listen to their answer, for they bear witness to Him. They testify concerning Him. *"The things concerning Jesus of Nazareth, which was a prophet, mighty in word and deed."*

He had been ridiculed, humiliated, beaten and crucified and now He is dead. Where did that leave them? They had the memory of Him, and they loved the memory of Him. They believed He had gone about doing good. They believed He meant well. They believed His ministry had been blessed, and they were walking on down that road with faith in Him and with love for Him still in their hearts.

Listen carefully now, and we can discover what it is that they lacked. They had lost their hope. They had lost their confidence that He could do all they thought He was going to do. Note the past tense. *"We had hoped that it was He which should redeem Israel."* Behind those words lies the attitude of disappointment and defeat. He meant well, but He didn't succeed. He tried, but He failed.

The hope that had burned within them has turned to smoldering ashes, but they love Him still. "He was a good man. He tried to do something, but He couldn't do it. He was a kind man. He was a prophet, mighty in word and deed. We had hoped He would redeem Israel and set up the Kingdom." Even now that hope is gone they won't speak an unkind word about Him, but instead of tarrying in Jerusalem they have struck out for Emmaus. Sadness lines their faces. There was no victory. There is no vision. There is no fervor or force. The fire is burning low.

Does this characterize the Church of Jesus Christ today? Does this characterize our own lives? Without question there are people everywhere who do believe in Jesus personally, but they aren't so sure of His ability to do what they hoped He would do. Everything seems to move so slowly, and almost without realizing it we become pessimistic.

Then we begin to compare Jesus with others. Perhaps the religion of Buddha would be more suited to us today. Perhaps the New Age movement better defines the thinking of our time. Slowly but surely our passion is cooling. We are losing our first love! It's not that we are less loyal to Jesus Christ, but that we are somehow unsure.

It is easy to lose the clear vision of Christ that brings joy and gladness to our hearts, that buoys up our spirits and makes our hearts burn with passion and love. That's what was happening to these two men who were traveling on that road to Emmaus. Let us take note of how Christ dealt with them.

Even today as we look back over all the centuries that have passed I find myself astonished that Jesus appeared to these men. Listen to His own words concerning them; *"O foolish men, and slow of heart to believe."* He knew their hearts, and that is His estimate of them; foolish men and slow to believe! Yet they are the very ones He comes to! He comes to them. He joins up with them. He walks with them, and He stirs their hearts to flame!

Jesus should never cease to astound us! We should never lose our sense of amazement at all that He is doing. If we will simply keep our eyes on Him, He will always be confounding us. We should watch for His sudden encounters every day! That is the grace of God in action. That is a revelation of the strength of His love for us. That shows us the tenderness of His heart.

Why does He come? Why does He seek us out? He comes seeking our love! In these hearts that held the shadow of doubt, He never the less recognized their love, and He came to them in order to renew it. Jesus always seeks what is beautiful, and He looks for the beautiful in places we would never think of looking. He sees spiritual qualities that our eyes cannot see.

He knows our hearts. He knows when we are losing our hope in Him. He knows when the fire of our love for Him and our commitment to Him is slowly dying, but He can see what remains; and He comes seeking that. He comes to strengthen what remains.

Jesus understood that the confidence of Cleopas and his companion had been shaken, and the hope they felt had been abandoned; but He also saw the loyalty to Him that remained. He came to them and He joined Himself to them in order to fan the flame that still remained on the altar of their hearts.

How did He do it? Mark this well. He did it by giving them a new perspective of familiar things. He did it by offering them a new interpretation. He made their hearts burn within them by talking to them. Their hearts did not burn while they talked to one another about Him. Their hearts did not burn while they talked to Him. Their hearts burned when He talked to them!

The fire was not rekindled as they questioned. It was not rekindled in the pouring out of their complaints. It was kindled when they quit talking and started listening. *"Were not our hearts burning within us, while He spoke to us in the way?"*

What did He say? He didn't tell them anything new. It was the old, old story; but they heard it as they had never heard it before. *"Beginning with Moses and all the Prophets he interpreted to them in the Scriptures the things concerning himself."*

He talked to them about Scripture that they were completely familiar with. They had been instructed in these Scriptures since childhood; ancient history and law and the prophets. He showed them how all those pathways culminated in Jesus of Nazareth; the man whose loss they were mourning.

They did not know Who they were talking to, but they were seeing new meaning in those old familiar words.

He talked, and they were quiet. A new vision of truth broke over them; and they found new understanding in things they had long known.

Just what was "the burning heart?" It was the joy of discovering their Lord in a new way. It was an awareness of their failure to rightly appreciate Him in the past. It was the knowledge that their lives were being set on a new path that would give them new power and take them to victory.

Now understand this. All this happened when they listened. It happened when He spoke to them. This is one of the greatest needs of this hour. As we listen, He will strengthen the things that remain.

In *Revelation 3:1-3* we read:

"I know your deeds; you have a reputation of being alive, but you are dead. Wake up! Strengthen what remains and is about to die, for I have not found your deeds complete in the sight of my God. Remember, therefore, what you have received and heard; obey it and repent. But if you do not wake up, I will come like a thief, and you will not know at what time I will come to you."

What are those things that remain? The love we have for Christ. The loyalty we have for Him. The doctrines that we hold true. The ordinances of the church. The routines of our days and weeks. The things that we hold in our hearts, but have lost excitement for and commitment to.

We need for these things to catch fire with new meaning. We need to be able to see clearly. We need to catch a passionate vision that drives us forward into creative action!

When this class first formed there was a young woman just out of college and newly married who was part of our Bible study. Her husband was on staff at our church. Sometimes it seemed to me that she was afraid of everything! She always asked for special prayer if the weather was threatening. If her husband was out of town at such a time she would walk the floor for hours, unable to sleep until the weather front had passed.

We rejoiced at news of their first pregnancy, and then their second. By their third they were sensing a new call on their life. They caught an entirely new vision!

Her husband accepted a position with a mission group that would take them to other parts of the world. We were amazed to see the zeal with which they approached this assignment. They sold all they had, and left behind friends and family as they were driven forward by the force of that call. This woman has become one of the bravest people I know. She has led short term mission assignments around the world. They are rearing their children in a challenging environment. Through the work of the Holy Spirit they heard the old, old story in a brand new way, and it held new meaning for them.

We have all seen this played out in the lives of others, and we have experienced it in our lives as well. God's call is not always to foreign countries, for a mission field surrounds us wherever we are. The Holy Spirit calls us, and the fire within us burns brightly as we hear His voice and answer His call.

I think it is safe to say that all of us need more stillness, more silence, and more listening for the voice of Jesus. There is great danger that in attempting to discuss Him and in attempting to serve Him we fail to remember that He is beyond the grasp of our intellect. The fires burn low while we discuss Him. The fires burn low while we learn about Him. The fires burn low while we attempt to do His work. What we need is to sit quietly with Him.

Some of you may be asking, how practical is this? People don't hear Him today the way they did in Bible times. Are you serious? Are we really supposed to listen for Him? How do we do this?

I became interested in spending quiet time with God many years ago through the writings of Madame

Guyon. She lived in France from 1648 to 1717. There were not many books in print at that time, and most of the population was illiterate. In seeking a way for the common person to communicate with God, she encouraged that quiet time be spent with Him. She encouraged people to just get still and clear their minds. She taught them to quiet their thoughts. She told them not to seek anything, but to rest in the sweetness of God's presence. She suggested simply saying, "Father, I am here with You; and I am listening." Furthermore, she emphasized that you would not always hear God's voice, but you would always be blessed by His presence.

This practice has been very meaningful to me. In the days before James retired he would come home from long days at work completely worn out. When I heard his pickup pull into the driveway I would begin to pray that as he entered our home he would sense the peace and presence of God. Many afternoons he would come in and we would go straight to the den and sit down in our chairs. Sometime we would not say a word for a long time. Sometimes we would fall asleep, but I began to understand in a new way the pure joy of James' presence. That helped me understand in a new way the joy of experiencing God's presence.

One evening when Mother was living with us I had tucked her into bed, and James was also down for the night. I sat down for quiet time with God. I remember saying, "Father, I am here, and I am listening." Immediately these words formed in my mind: " I will strengthen you. I will help you. I will uphold you with my righteous right hand." Of course, these words are from *Isaiah 41:10*. They are words of comfort, but I did not understand why those words were given to me. Life seemed to be moving along quite comfortably! In some perplexity I said, "Thank You, Lord. That's nice to be reminded of." Little did I know that within hours Mother would take a turn that would move her out of our home and into assisted living. In the time that lay ahead for her I often remembered those precious words. They were given to me when I got still and listened.

It is not true that God does not speak to us as He did in olden times. It is true that we don't wait to hear Him as they did then. Our lives are surrounded by noise. We are wrapped in noise! Many people turn on their television or their radio before they get out of bed in the morning. I know people who leave their radio or TV on all night. They can't sleep without the noise. When we get into our cars we turn on the radio or a CD. When we walk into our homes we flip on the TV.

Test yourself by any day in your life. Can you honestly hear God? Of course you can! How long have you taken to be quiet and listen to Him? Listen! Listen in the early morning. Listen in the midst of other voices. Listen! Listen!! Listen!!!

No one who cultivates the habit of listening will ever be disappointed. We will be aware of renewed strength, and of fresh power. The fire that burns within will drive us onward and upward in the one-of-a-kind path of service to which we are called.

Oh, that we would know more burning of heart! Our Christian principles and our programs and our religious routines and our seminars and the machinery of it all can overwhelm us. May we take time to listen, that by His interpretation the things we do will flame with fire and light. May a Holy Passion rise up within us that commits us to the coming of His Kingdom in our hearts, in our homes, within our families, in our churches, in our city, and in the whole wide world. May God give us ears to hear and hearts to respond to His Holy Spirit, for His name's sake. Amen and amen.

El Shaddai, My Adoni
(The Strong One, My Lord)

El Shaddai, my Adonai,
Holy is Your name on High.
You're the Promised One revealed.
By Your wounds my soul is healed.
You're the Rock, to You I cling.
From You Living Water springs.

You're the Blessed One of Zion.
You're Messiah, Judah's Lion.
Jehovah Jireh; the Great I am.
You're my Savior, God's perfect lamb.

You're my strength, my sun and shield,
To Your Spirit will I yield.
You're my song, my everything;
To You my life, my love I bring.

El Shaddai; my Adonai,
I exalt You God most high.
King of Kings, my El Shaddai,
Lord of Lords, my Adonai!

Think On These Things

Would you say that your heart burns within you with love for Jesus Christ? Explain your answer.

I wonder how often Jesus joins us, and we fail to recognize Him. In looking back over your life, can you describe a time when that was true for you? Think over the times of perplexity; times when circumstances were not what you expected. That may provide you with some clues.

What do you have of Jesus today? What do you believe about Him? How far does your faith in Him go?

Are there things you hoped He would do that have not come to pass? Are there issues over which hope has been lost?

How are you responding to those things?

What do you think Jesus' estimate of you is?

Why does He still come to us? What does He do in His coming?

In response to Him, what are we called to do? When did you last sit quietly and simply listen for His voice? When did you last sit quietly and rest in the wonder of His presence and of His love?

I think you will enjoy reading and thinking about *Philippians 3:1-16.*

The Prayer For Spiritual Life

God, I admit that I'm not perfect and that I have sinned.

Many times, I have gone my own way instead of Your way.

Please forgive me for all of my sins.

Thank You, Jesus, for dying on the cross

to pay the penalty for my sins.

Come into my life and

make me the person You want me to be.

Thank You, Jesus, for what You will do

in me, to me, and through me.

In Your holy name, I pray. Amen.

If you were sincere in praying The Prayer For Spiritual Life[1], God promises you eternal life.

"I tell you the truth, whoever hears my word and believes him who sent me has eternal life and will not be condemned, he has crossed over from death to life."
John 5:24

Acknowledgments

Praise and honor be to our God, who daily reveals the truth of His word to those who diligently seek Him.

It is with deep gratitude that I express my appreciation to the following for their contributions:

To my daughter, Lauren LoRe, who surprised me by moving forward to get these manuscripts published.

To my daughter, Lynn Talley, who helped me with the discussion questions that appear at the end of each chapter.

To my friend, Alice Michie, who freely gave of her sound wisdom and sharp insight.

To Becky Khani for her assistance in editing.

To Michael Tutone, who worked toward putting the manuscript in order for publication.

To Kathleen Fritsche, who through editing brought the project to completion and who designed the book cover.

To our Thursday Bible Study. Over many years these women have challenged me with their intellects and encouraged me by their determination to know our Lord and Savior better. Thank you for every phone call, every note, and every word of encouragement that you have brought me over the past 3 years. The project could not have been completed without your faithful prayer support.

Notes

Are You Living Out of Your Flesh or Out of Your Spirit? – Adapted from the work of G. Campbell Morgan, *The Westminster Pulpit*, Vol. IV (Westwood, N.J., Fleming H. Revell Co., 1954), pp. 97-109.

The Ultimate Test of Christianity – Adapted from the work of G. Campbell Morgan, T*he Westminster Pulpit*, Vol. IV (Westwood, N.J., Fleming H. Revell Co., 1954), pp. 110-122.

The Day of Pentecost: Tongues Like Fire – Adapted from the work of G. Campbell Morgan, T*he Westminster Pulpit*, Vol. VII (Westwood, N.J., Fleming H. Revell Co., 1954), pp. 142–154.

The Holy Spirit Has Come! – Adapted from the work of G. Campbell Morgan, *The Westminster Pulpit*, Vol. VI (Westwood, N.J., Fleming H. Revell Co., 1954), pp. 127-139.

Filled With The Holy Spirit – Adapted from the work of G. Campbell Morgan, *The Westminster Pulpit*, Vol. VIII (Westwood, N.J., Fleming H. Revell Co., 1954), pp. 181-193.

What If I Do Not Have The Holy Spirit? – Adapted from the work of G. Campbell Morgan, T*he Westminster Pulpi*t, Vol. I (Westwood, N.J., Fleming H. Revell Co., 1954), pp. 230–241.

The Spirit of Life – Adapted from the work of G. Campbell Morgan, *The Westminster Pulpit*, Vol. I (Westwood, N.J., Fleming H. Revell Co., 1954), pp. 180-189.

The Witness of The Holy Spirit – Adapted from the work of G. Campbell Morgan, *The Westminster Pulpit*, Vol. I (Westwood N.J., Fleming H. Revell Co., 1954), pp. 153–165.

The Fruit of The Spirit – Adapted from the work of G. Campbell Morgan, *The Westminster Pulpit*, Vol. I (Westwood, N.J. Fleming H. Revell Co., 1954), pp. 166–179.

Do Our Hearts Burn Within Us? – Adapted from the work of G. Campbell Morgan, *The Westminster Pulpit*, Vol. I (Westwood, N.J. Fleming H. Revell Co., 1954) pp. 85-96.

The Prayer For Spiritual Life – June Hunt, *Caring for a Loved One with Cancer*[1], (Copyright 2011 by Hope For The Heart, Inc., Published by Crossway), pp. 104-105.

Blessings of The Holy Spirit

"This book challenges you to examine you to examine yourself and think deeper about the role of the Holy Spirit in your life. I like how Marjorie Jackson explains the original meanings of the words in the text and then applies these truths to your every day affairs! I especially like reading the sections about her friends and family. I highly recommend this book to anyone!"

— E. McKee, Hudson Oaks, Texas

"Beautifully written, well-researched practical study of the Holy Spirit with discussion questions included. This makes it a wonderful, ready-made tool for a bible study or for an individual or group! It is a deep and satisfying read that can be life changing."

— Robert M. Hansard, Fort Worth, Texas

"Marjorie Jackson's understanding of Biblical truth and God's Word on this topic is refreshing. Her teaching provides clarity as well as inspiration for daily living. Thankful for this teaching on the Holy Spirit."

— Kathy Burr, Fort Worth, Texas

"I have read many books on this subject. Here you will see how the coming of the Holy Spirit was the culmination of Jesus' earthly mission and you will understand the crucial importance of receiving the Holy Spirit into your life. I highly recommend this book."

— Joann Slay, Haltom City, Texas

Made in the USA
Columbia, SC
17 March 2020